Healing
Scarred
Hearts

Healing Scarred Hearts

A Family's Story of Addiction,
Loss, and Finding Light

Susán Hoemke

BROWN BOOKS
PUBLISHING GROUP

© 2018 Susán Hoemke

Healing Scarred Hearts
A Family's Story of Addiction, Loss, and Finding Light

Brown Books Publishing Group
16250 Knoll Trail Drive, Suite 205
Dallas, Texas 75248
www.BrownBooks.com
(972) 381-0009

A New Era in Publishing®

Publisher's Cataloging-In-Publication Data

Names: Hoemke, Susán.
Title: Healing scarred hearts : a family's story of addiction, loss, and finding light / Susán Hoemke.
Description: Dallas, Texas : Brown Books Publishing Group, [2018]
Identifiers: ISBN 9781612549880
Subjects: LCSH: Hoemke, Susán--Family. | Parents of drug addicts. | Drug addicts--Family relationships. | Opioid abuse. | Loss (Psychology) | Life change events.
Classification: LCC HV5805.H64 A3 2018 | DDC 362.29/9--dc23

ISBN 978-1-61254-988-0
LCCN 2017958497

Printed in the United States
10 9 8 7 6 5 4 3 2 1

For more information or to contact the author, please go to
www.HealingScarredHearts.com.

To everyone who loves or has lost someone battling addiction,
let the healing begin . . .

God grant me the serenity

to accept the things I cannot change;

courage to change the things I can;

and wisdom to know the difference.

Contents

Acknowledgments

Thank you to my husband, children, family, and friends for all of their love and support as we remember our dear Hayden. We know he would want this story told in the hopes of easing others' pain. I would like to send a special thank-you to my editor, Darla Bruno, who shaped and guided my manuscript on professional and personal levels. I would also like to recognize Shea Barakatt and her contribution to the book that sheds light on many questions asked by families in need of support. Last but not least, an abundance of gratitude to the Brown Books Publishing Group for understanding and embracing our story, believing it should be shared.

—1—

Why

We must be willing to get rid of the life we've planned,
so as to have the life that is waiting for us.
—JOSEPH CAMPBELL

People make plans and have expectations for how their lives will be lived, with hopes and dreams for the future. We assume if we make good choices and are good people everything should fall into place. We can easily get caught up in our "bubbles," believing all is well, and have a sense of pride about ourselves. Our family was living this way until our steady, comfortable world was shaken, and we spent eight long years living two lives, it seemed. Living as the family we expected to be and living as a family with dark secrets, hoping to not be judged. We tried to keep home life normal, but we were forced to walk in a darkness we did not understand—a darkness that was as foreign as living on another planet and not knowing if we would survive. The "being" we raised, loved, and would have given our lives for became a stranger at times. Who could we turn to? And who was this "alien" person we no longer recognized and could not understand? It seemed as if we were living with split personalities. On good days, our oldest son was pleasant and joyful, and we would talk about his day and share our thoughts. When Hayden spoke, I always listened and enjoyed his company because we shared the same humor and I could relate to him. We had a bond I felt could never be broken. But as he got older, changes, physically as well as mentally, began to occur. He was not sure how to deal with his desire to feel different and less anxious. His curiosity and lack of understanding spiraled into substance experimentation at a young age. Our lack of knowledge on drug abuse and mental conditions blinded us from the sad reality happening right before us.

As the years passed and we finally understood Hayden needed much help, his journey to get help began. Hearing him called an addict for the first time was unbelievable to us and to him. As the years passed and his changed behavior became intense, from simply trying drugs to risking his life for them, we started to believe and learn what it meant to be an addict. Addiction is a disease, and he would battle it for the rest of his life, even with tools and support. If his mind was not kept busy, he would start to thirst for harmful substances and go on a mission to find them. Addicts have to have a full schedule and no extra time to sit around and think, because the inner core of the brain takes over and addicts begin to feel desperate, like being severely dehydrated and in need of water, except the need they feel is for drugs. After getting the substance he desired and using it, the changes began, and his eyes appeared heavy and red, so that it eventually appeared as if he had no eyes at all, when he collapsed onto his bed. His pleasant voice became a low slur, and at night his mind seemed to wander and play tricks on him. He stayed away as much as possible and hid in the darkness. Hours would pass before we saw him emerge from behind his closed door. Many late nights, we were awakened by this person we did not seem to know anymore, as our bedroom lights would flip on and he would come to the side of our bed to tell us he was hearing people outside or he had just discovered someone was watching him through his computer camera. Sometimes he claimed to hear shotgun fire and believed he was being hunted. At times, he would seem like a scared child again. He could be easily confused and irritated, not knowing what to believe. He lost his self-esteem and disliked who he had become. Substance abuse had changed everything about him.

Often, we hoped he would just fall asleep and not wake until morning, but on rare occasions, and with horrible guilt, I hoped he would not wake at all. Every day became a mystery, but we continued to try and bring as much light to it as we could. We would send him away for help and then he would come back, over and over. Life would go on, but the impact on the family was extreme. We continued our daily routines and hobbies, along with church and family vacations, and we always wore our smiles and hoped no one would notice the pain and concern we had for the whole family. From the confusion, we could see signs of distress through our other children, and this offered its own challenges. As time went by, the destruction was slowly building, and the devastation of living with this stranger was taking its toll on all of us.

Hayden's disease was consuming him like a starving serpent, and we felt helpless, even though we were constantly working to "fix" him. One day we were the enablers living in denial, pretending all would be fine, and the next day we were loud and demanding, reminding him of the rules. We lived in waves of good times and bad during these trying years.

Hayden would yell profanities at times, which was completely out of his nature and made him seem more like a stranger. We began to wonder what we'd done wrong and ask ourselves if we were bad parents. The guilt and pain of watching him struggle led us to tears. His behavior was bizarre and unbelievable. Our bright boy was slowly entering a darkness.

Hayden had a big imagination and lots of creativity. His sense of humor kept us all laughing at times. The side of him we knew best was the loving, funny one with hopes and dreams, full of energy and a love for music. He would pass out hugs and fist bumps while making jokes and crazy comments. Everyone who met him liked him, and he had no enemies, it seemed. He was a popular kid and was always surrounded with friends. Because of his creativity, he could tell a great story about where his dreams took him at night when he slept. His favorite dreams were the ones in which he could fly free and soar above the clouds, going wherever he wanted with his arms open wide and the wind blowing through his hair. Hayden, a free spirit, lived moment to moment and rarely looked to the future. He mostly wore a smile growing up in his younger years, never causing us any trouble, and therefore we had big hopes and dreams for him. As proud parents, we expected a bright future for him.

We were completely ignorant and unprepared for what was to come and for the darkness that would overtake our son Hayden. We were challenged beyond normal physical, emotional, and mental boundaries. Every day became a battle, and it felt at times like we were at war with a strategic enemy. We were forced to learn the hard way, but we began to understand there were many families like us longing for the son or daughter they once knew to return to them. All of us wanted answers and constantly asked why, but we were left with endless uncertainty. The battle against the disease of addiction and its impact on the family forever scars the heart.

—2—

First Born/Early Years

*. . . Incontestable fact that sleep
creates favorable conditions for telepathy.*
—SIGMUND FREUD, "DREAMS AND TELEPATHY"

1990. I'm pregnant and we are going to be parents! What an amazing year for us.

Carl, my husband, and I were high school sweethearts, and after five years of marriage, we began our family. Being a mom meant everything to me. I dreamed about being a mom since I was a little girl. We wanted many children, and I was loaded with love and ready for a houseful. We learned that our firstborn would be a son, and we could not have been more excited. His due date was late July 1991, so for the full nine months, I ate right, exercised, and stayed well for our beautiful baby to have the best chance to be born heathy. I felt so great and alive from the excitement. We bought some baby-name books and spent days finding the right name to call him. I took the books to work with me so I could read every day until a name had been chosen. Finally, a definition read: "Get this boy pin-striped diapers and a *Wall Street Journal.*" Carl and I both loved the name and really liked the professional spin this particular book had on the description. He would be Hayden and have two middle names to keep the family tradition—Hayden Richard Edward. His two middle names were after his uncle and grandfather.

We began planning his room and shopping for adorable bedding sets and a crib. I fell in love with the white, navy blue, baby blue, and red sailboat theme. When his room was complete, I sat in there rocking and listening to the little baby mobile that hung above his crib and played a sweet lullaby.

Everything was in place and ready for our sweet child to come home. The months passed, and the joy of feeling Hayden's every move as I would talk and sing to him was amazing. Carl and I attended the prenatal training classes and spent many hours dreaming of the day our little Hayden would arrive. We watched the video that was recorded during our sonogram, of little Hayden inside my womb, several times. It was fascinating to observe our child kicking and punching while still in my belly. We felt confident that we had everything figured out and felt ready to be parents.

The time had come at week thirty-four to meet our little guy. As I went into labor, Carl rushed me to the hospital so we could meet our new little baby boy. After a long night on July 27, 1991, our son arrived full of life and energy. Oh, he was beautiful, with small features, blue eyes, and blond hair, and he weighed 7 pounds, 1 ounce. He was actually very bald, but what little hair he had was blond. When they laid him in my arms, it seemed unbelievable to be looking him in the eyes. I studied his every feature and listened to him breathe and loved when his tiny fingers grasped my hand. It was beautiful to watch Carl lean down with his big arms and scoop up little Hayden, cradling him with love and joy. Carl even changed the first poopy diaper, and that was impressive! We were officially parents.

We drove home the next day to get Hayden settled into his room and begin our new life. We already loved being parents and had a sense of pride we had never felt before. As the months passed, we began to learn how much time and effort went into being new parents, but we loved it. We had many friends who also started families, so we all shared advice and stories. We had wonderful birthday parties, many play dates, and the holidays were amazing with all his new little toys underneath the tree. What a blessing it was to sit by the Christmas tree and read '*Twas the Night Before Christmas* to Hayden as he lay in my arms gazing up at me in his little Christmas pajamas. I would sing "Silent Night" softly and rock him to sleep.

When Hayden was two years old, Carl got a new job that moved us to Austin, away from all friends and family. I'd never lived out of the town I was born in, so this was going to be a big adventure, especially with a toddler. Carl's new job had him traveling many days a week, which left Hayden and me alone together most of the time. He became my world, and we explored every day, taking in new sights and trying new places to eat. We visited the zoo on occasion and any art museums or malls I could find. He loved to play in the swimming pool and quickly learned to swim.

The first several months of living in our new town were very hard on me, but Hayden brought me so much joy. He made me laugh and helped the days pass quickly until Carl would arrive home. Hayden began speaking at a very young age, so we talked a lot. He was my little buddy, and eventually we began visiting a church nearby and making new friends. A group of us went to the park at least once a week, so we quickly got to know other kids Hayden's age. Life began to feel more comfortable. At the end of the day, Hayden loved to hold a piece of my hair as I said a prayer and rocked him to sleep at night, which strengthened the beautiful bond between us. When Carl arrived home, he and Hayden spent hours together playing, and Hayden loved to sit on his big shoulders. Four months passed, and we decided Hayden needed a backyard to play in, so we began looking for a new home. We moved out of our apartment and into a house in a new neighborhood after the first six-month apartment lease was over. Carl and I were planning for more kids, and after a few more months passed, we broke the news to Hayden that he was going to be a big brother, and he was so happy. When Hayden was three in 1994, our second son, Landon, arrived, and then would come Miranda in 1996. They all played so well together and were so much fun. Olivia arrived six years afterward in the spring of 2002 and was our wonderful surprise child.

Our plans were falling into place, and we were so proud of our family. And then I began to have dreams about Hayden and losing him somehow in bizarre ways. Like most moms, the fear of losing a child is just in the back of your mind, and you tell yourself to stop having crazy thoughts. When Hayden was about ten years old, I had a very vivid dream that was in color, and I can still see it in my head today.

First Dream: White Wolf

I began looking for Hayden outside and found myself in the backyard of his grandparents' house playing near the alleyway. He was always exploring and wandering off to see what adventure he could find. He was about ten years old and full of life. My heart sank as I came around the corner of the house to see Hayden standing and staring at a huge white wolf, just at the end of the long, narrow alley. As I began to run toward Hayden and call out to him to flee from the danger, I could see the large mouth of the wolf opening to expose its great, white teeth. I was running but not moving closer to him. It was as if I was on an elliptical machine going nowhere. I watched as the wolf lunged at Hayden, putting his mouth around Hayden's entire torso. The wolf was trying to swallow him up, and it started to run away with Hayden hanging like a rag doll from his jaw's grasp. I stood there, feeling hopeless, not knowing what to do. My eyes flew open, and I had a sick feeling inside as I awoke. I told Carl about it, and we were both so glad it was just a dream. The kids loved stories, and whenever any of us had dreams we could remember, we would share them with each other. When I shared mine that morning we all agreed it was scary, but I never forgot it and wondered why it remained so vivid in my mind.

When Hayden was ten, we moved from Austin to Highland Park, Texas, which is a suburb of Dallas. Carl was offered a great job with a large corporation in downtown Dallas and could not pass up the opportunity. We spent many days touring and deciding where we would live and what schools our kids would go to. After much research, we bought a house in the highly sought-after neighborhood, Highland Park. It had great schools and many opportunities for our kids to get involved. The area was beautiful, with nice homes, lovely parks, and beautiful shrubs and flowers at every corner. It all seemed perfect for us, and the kids were excited about the move. We were so happy and began making friends and enjoying the shopping and great restaurants. The area had an annual neighborhood parade every Fourth of July, and we attended to watch the decorated cars, bikes, and floats. Everyone lined chairs up along the street so when the candy was thrown, their kids would get a bag full. Our kids were happy and adjusting well to the move. Each of them got involved in some type of sport, and this consumed many hours on the weekend, but Carl and I loved sports and activities. Watching the kids grow up was an amazing time, and we were busy loving life.

The year was 2004 when I had the second dream about Hayden, and the next morning I shared it with my husband and kids.

SECOND DREAM: THE SERPENT

My surroundings were unfamiliar. The sky was dim and gray, and all around me was thick green rainforest. It felt so real and seemed so clear, like I was really there. The colors were so vivid and seemed so realistic. I was standing and talking to an unknown person whose face was never revealed to me. Hayden was with me but off playing in the distance, being the curious one he always was, burning off the extra energy by exploring. I remember glancing over at him a few times to be sure he was okay while still in conversation with the faceless unknown source. As I turned to look one more time, I saw that Hayden had picked up a large stick and was testing it out on an old, weathered, three-sided shed covered in lush green vines and trees. On his third thrust upward to see what was above him, I had a strong sense of dread and yelled for him to stop. It was too late, and as the broken-down shed began to collapse around Hayden, a huge, unrecognizable, grotesque figure fell to the ground. As I began to run toward Hayden, my heart was pounding, and right before I reached him, the grotesque serpent/ demon swallowed him whole. I watched in horror and disbelief as the very long, wide serpent began to slide around me on its way to an unknown destination, with Hayden trapped inside, looking at me through the belly. Hayden was lying faceup with his eyes open and his arms crossed in front of him. The serpent was a grayish-green color, slick, and thick-skinned, but clear enough for me to see through it. It was an awful feeling. I stood almost in a trance, watching helplessly as he slowly slid by me. I knew Hayden was still alive yet being taken away from me. Completely consumed by something I did not understand.

I quickly woke and realized it was morning. I could not go back to sleep, so I got up to get some coffee. At the breakfast table that morning, I shared my dream with the family, and we all agreed it was creepy and strange, but of course it was just a dream. Carl and I had been happily married for eighteen years now, and we were still living in Highland Park, Texas. Carl had a wonderful job—we were all healthy; we had money; I was a stay-at-home mom; we were happy, attended church every Sunday, and had wonderful family support and connections on both sides of our families. Yes, life seemed perfect.

At thirteen, Hayden was a smart kid—straight-A student and involved in sports. Landon, two and a half years younger, was the quiet, more laid-back one—a sensitive, polite kid with a heart of gold. He was also very smart and was constantly creating and brainstorming about his bright future. He took up a love for computers, and math seemed to come easy for him. He was obsessed with football and was planning to go pro. Miranda talked early and was a strong-willed child. At the age of four, she fell in love with shoes and fashion, and by the age of five, she decided she would become a fashion designer. She was also becoming an amazing tumbler in the gym, and school came easy for her. She loved her big brothers dearly. Olivia was born six years after her sister Miranda. She was a sweet, congenial child who learned quickly from her big brothers and sister. She was a little angel, and now the family was complete. With Hayden in eighth grade, Landon in fifth, Miranda third, and Olivia in preschool, we felt just shy of the Brady Bunch. They all played together and spent time watching movies. The boys would hop on their bikes and ride to the park to hang out with friends. Our children were living the American dream in an upscale neighborhood with excellent schools and the best of everything around them. We took a family vacation every summer and spent holidays with extended family. My parents loved being grandparents and came down once a month to visit and help with the kids. They loved the kids and were always there if we needed them. I was always home when the kids got out of school and made sure to listen to any stories that might come home with them and check for homework. They were all involved in after-school activities, so like any other mom with a competitive spirit, I made sure everyone's schedule allowed them to do what they wanted to do.

Carl was hard at work to support the family and was traveling but home on the weekends to attend football games, dance recitals, soccer games, gymnastic competitions, etc. The kids looked up to him and loved him being home. Carl and I were oblivious and naive to a whole other dark world surrounding us. In high school, Carl did drink some on the weekends, but neither of us ever considered drugs. I was the good girl and stayed away from parties and drinking altogether because of respect for my parents and what I had been taught. The thought of getting in trouble made me cringe, and I liked being trustworthy. Carl and I met his senior year and my junior year of high school, then married one year after high school while attending Abilene Christian University. We were both attending college full time and working to support ourselves. We were planning our children's future before they even had a life. We had it all figured out, or so we thought.

Hayden successfully graduated from the eighth grade and would be going off to high school. Landon and Miranda would be at the middle school and little Olivia in preschool. We took our big family vacation in the summer just before school started. We took the kids to Jamaica and had a wonderful time. It was a trip to remember, and the kids were able to experience a different culture. Hayden had become a big fan of rap music and the whole rap-singer "look." He began wearing baggy clothes, large T-shirts, and flat-billed hats with large lettering on the front. It was the beginning of that new fad, so we just went with it and did not put too much thought into it. It did put a bit of a damper on the vacation because he was dressed too warm for the climate we were in. We argued a few times, but he wanted to wear those clothes, even though they made him feel hot and sweaty. This was his new identity, and he was very passionate about it. Slowly we began to notice a little change in Hayden's attitude, but he was in the first stages of puberty, so we brushed it off but reminded him that we expected a good attitude.

We heard raising teenagers could be challenging, but we were completely unprepared for what was to come.

Fall arrived and school was beginning again, and there was excitement in the air. We lived so close to all of the schools, which meant there was no bus system, so I took all of the kids to and from school every day, which gave us plenty of time to talk. The first month passed, and it was time for the homecoming football game and dance. This was Hayden's first time to ask a date, and they were going with a group of friends to all of the activities that night. Hayden looked so handsome wearing a dark navy-blue suit, and his tie matched his date's dress. As tradition, all of the parents met for pictures and admired each other's kids. A few parents took the group to drop them off at the school dance, and Hayden was going to be picked up later that night to spend the night at his friend's house.

Around 11:30 p.m., as the dance was ending, we received a call from Hayden and he did not sound very well. His words were a little slurred, and he was asking for a change of clothes because he'd forgotten his overnight bag. We thought he might be sick, so Carl grabbed what Hayden needed and headed to meet with him. Surprisingly, Hayden had been drinking. He had left the dance early with a few friends and his date to go hang out and drink at a friend's house. He had a new friend who lived within walking distance of the school, and his mother was a single mom and worked at night, which we were unaware of. We were surprised he was in this situation, because up to this time, we never had any trouble from him and it was his first dance. We brought him home and talked with him, keeping the punishment simple but clear about our expectations. Hayden was excused to his room, and Carl and I looked at each other shaking our heads. We agreed this was much earlier than we expected our kid to be drinking. I assumed we might deal with this issue during his senior year of high school, or even college, but never at this young age. This was the beginning of his and our family's struggles.

In the spring of 2005, Hayden's ninth-grade year, we received a call late at night from another parent. Hayden had become friends with a nice kid he'd met at school, and his family lived pretty close to us. They spent a lot of time together and enjoyed sports and getting together to hang out and play Xbox. Because time had passed from the earlier issue, where he had been drinking after the dance, we allowed Hayden to have a sleepover at his new friend's home and we were trusting him again. As I answered the phone, I heard a somewhat loud, concerned voice on the other end announcing, "Our oldest son has caught our boys smoking pot, and this is unacceptable to us!"

We were shocked to hear the news, and at first, we did not believe it. We wanted to give Hayden the benefit of the doubt and let him explain. After all, he knew how serious this was, didn't he?

Then I realized we'd never had a discussion about drug use, but it never occurred to us that we needed to. People who used drugs lived on the streets in dark alleys, came from lower income families, and had no parental guidance, so I thought. The news was not talking about drug abuse, teachers were not talking about it, churches were not talking about it, politicians were not, and none of our friends or family members were either. On occasion, we might see something in a movie or TV show, but the subject of drug abuse really seemed to be taboo. In the past, because alcoholism was present in both sides of the family, we briefly talked with our kids about drinking and the dangers of starting young but not of any other form of drug use.

We went and picked Hayden up that night to bring him home. He admitted that another friend gave them some pot to try and he was curious about it. But he said he felt stupid and was sorry. We shared our thoughts and what we knew about the seriousness of his actions and told him pot was illegal as well. We told him our expectations and let him know if this happened again we would take his cell phone and he would be grounded. His punishment was to be homebound for the weekend, which he was upset about, but he nodded his head that he understood, stayed polite, and said again he was stupid for doing it. But by the next day, his attitude changed a bit and he wanted to go out with friends. He became a little angry as we held to our punishment agreement, went upstairs, and slammed the door. This made for an unpleasant weekend, but we knew it was necessary.

—3—

Keeping Life "Normal"

Hayden finished his ninth-grade year and summer arrived. His grades dropped a bit from the straight As we were used to, but we knew high school was more challenging and were not concerned. The other three kids were doing great and looking forward to a fun summer. Landon played football and spent much of the summer practicing and playing with friends. He dreamed of the NFL someday after college and was into collecting sports cards. He mostly wore football jerseys and baseball caps with his favorite teams across the front. He was our quiet one and enjoyed being by himself, building new projects or taking electronics apart to see how they worked. He was a great student who loved math and computers. Miranda was our gymnast and could whip out a backflip. For her, though, fashion was first, and it was all about shoes and cute outfits. She was a smart girl and also doing very well in school. Olivia was taking everything in and admired each of her siblings. She talked early and was always happy-go-lucky. She loved playing with Miranda, and they would spend hours together.

With summer, however, came new challenges. I was beginning to find items I was not familiar with in Hayden's room. I would find small squares of very thin white paper. Sometimes they would be on his desk and other times in his pockets, and I would find them while I was doing laundry. I asked him what they were for, and he quickly said, "Oh, I was just making projects and writing on them." At first, that made sense to me.

As more time passed, I would find lighters in his pockets and then eye drops began showing up. One night, I couldn't sleep, and I got up to use the bathroom. It was dark, so I could not see, but I could definitely smell. I stopped walking to try to focus on what odor was in the air. I had smelled pot once or twice when we had gone to concerts, so I knew that smell. I began asking myself if it was marijuana. *Oh my gosh, I thought. Where is that coming from?*

I went from our bedroom around the corner into the family room to look out the window into the backyard. I peered into the darkness and no one was out there, but a figure upstairs was hanging halfway out of Hayden's window, puffing away on a joint. I squinted harder and pressed my face up to the glass for a better look. It was Hayden! I stepped back in shock and turned to head up the stairs to his bedroom. I reached for the doorknob and realized the door was locked. I began knocking, trying not to wake the other kids up. After a few minutes, he opened the door—after flushing his joint down the toilet. His eyes were red and puffy. I was furious that he was smoking again and that he brought this illegal substance into our home! He received strong words from me and did not deny what I was saying. I took his cell phone, ordered him to bed, and I crawled back into bed as Carl was waking and asking what was going on. After I explained, he sighed heavily and said we would talk to him in the morning so he could receive his punishment.

The next day, we shared our disappointment in him and reminded him of the trouble marijuana could get him into, because it was illegal as well as harmful and not worth the risk. He agreed and said he was sorry again, but now we had some doubt he really was. We became a little concerned and bought a motivational book for him to read as well as one about harmful drugs. Time passed, he served his punishment, and he seemed better. But it was just a matter of time before more items showed up, and he was in more trouble. I began to think and reflect back on the "contracts" that Hayden signed at school to stay drug-free, along with door decorating, crazy sock day, and the many fun activities the kids participated in during drug-awareness week to understand how harmful drugs are, and something did not seem right about this approach. Were kids learning anything they really needed to know about drugs, or did they see this as a fun week?

A new school year was beginning, and we were busy checking schedules, buying supplies, and shopping for school clothes. The excitement of back-to-school was in the air. Despite Hayden's issues, we were trying to keep life as normal as possible for our three other children. We were trying to balance school, homework, sports, and activities, and play dates, attend church, host birthday parties and holiday gatherings, and take family vacations. It was hard to do this, because there was just one unexpected surprise after another. Besides Hayden trying to hide his drug use and having issues at school, his addiction was aiding in poor choices, which began getting him into trouble with the law.

One evening, I made dinner for the three younger ones, because Hayden left the house with a friend to "go do homework" and at the time seemed to be doing fine. My youngest was four years old, and I was putting her to sleep when the phone rang. I answered, and a police officer began telling me he had my son sitting in his squad car because he was with a friend who was buying marijuana. It did not surprise me, however, to hear the officer say how nice Hayden seemed, and he was being congenial, therefore I could just come pick him up. So, I tucked my sweet children into bed and left Landon in charge because Carl was away on business. Miranda knew something was wrong, but I tried to minimize the situation and kissed her good night. When I arrived to pick up Hayden at about 9:30 p.m. in the dark of night, lights were flashing and I could see him sitting in the back of the police car.

I just couldn't believe my kid was sitting in a police car, and my heart sank. The officer spoke with me and let me know the part of town I was in had a few suspected drug houses, even though I was just a five-minute drive away from the other side of the major freeway. Million-dollar homes on one side and drug dealers on the other. *There is no safe place*, I remember thinking for the first time. I asked the officer why they couldn't shut down the houses if they knew which ones were dealing drugs. He reminded me they have to be caught in the act of dealing drugs or there was nothing they could do.

Anyone who first met Hayden always liked him, so the officer gave him a firm talk and released him to me that night. I remember crying and being very upset; Hayden was scared and told me he was so sorry again. He wanted us to believe he just happened to be in the car when his friend went to make that purchase and did not know where he was going.

Even though he was struggling, he kept his popularity at school with friends. We really liked the group of kids he normally hung out with, and they would come over sometimes. They were usually all polite, and on occasion, ate dinner at our house, but he had other friends who continued to experiment with drugs. He could always manage to keep it together when in trouble with us, using his unique sense of humor so we would give him the benefit of the doubt. We continued believing he was being in the wrong place at the wrong time and that his phase of troubles would pass. After all, we were good parents and starting to understand teenagers, so we thought. We still had three more would-be teens, so the more I could learn now, the better.

Many times, the firstborn kid is looked up to by their siblings and can make a good or bad impact. The other kids loved Hayden, and he could easily get their attention when he walked into the room because he was entertaining. Therefore, I was trying to keep his issues and troubles quiet. I wanted him to be a good example, not a bad one, and I began to feel that more was going on with Hayden, but I just could not figure it out.

He became secretive and started closing his door as soon as he got home. He seemed distracted and disconnected from the family as time went on, and he was losing interest in school and sports. His grades continued to slip, and he was struggling with completing assignments. We hired a tutor to come to the house twice a week to help him with his schoolwork.

I continued to talk with him and make sure our relationship was strong, so if he needed any more support, he would feel comfortable telling me. He did tell me he was done with lacrosse and did not want to play anymore. He lost interest in sports and wanted to focus on music, as he was hoping to be a rapper. I was disappointed and knew being a professional rapper was not going to happen, and it actually made me irritated, but I thought about the promise I made to myself. If our kids found a passion, we would support it. So, I put a smile on my face, and we discussed his thoughts about music and writing. I knew he could write well because he made good grades in English and was very creative. He also had a decent voice, so I tried to be encouraging, but his attitude continued to change as the months passed, and I felt he was pulling away from our relationship. I attributed all this to puberty and finding his independence, but so much began to happen so fast.

As I began to pay closer attention to details in hopes for more understanding about Hayden, I found myself on my hands and knees again, crawling around like a detective looking for evidence at a murder scene, digging through his desk drawers and lifting up the mattress to peer underneath, checking for items Hayden should not have possessed. I climbed to the top of the closet to lift and move everything that might be hiding clues to the strange behavior, usually linked with drug abuse, that Hayden seemed to have again. I knew there had to be something we were missing. I started to find small, clear bags that looked like something you got buttons in when you bought new clothes. I found them in his jeans pockets and desk drawers along with more eye drops and lighters, which began to make sense for the strange smells on his clothing, and small, empty bottles.

In the dark of night, I prowled around my own home, making my way up the stairs to find Hayden's cell phone so I could check his texts for evidence if something more was going on. I would push open his door and disconnect his phone from the wall to take it downstairs with me to go through his texts. Carl would also spend time reading through his messages to see if we could make sense of the unknown. My stomach would knot, and it would feel as if it were being squeezed like a sponge. The text messages were vague, but it seemed as if he was communicating with more than just his friends. I would talk to him and he would deny anything was going on. He would say, "Mom, I'm fine," and that the items I was finding were old stuff he was not using. I would feel guilty for being suspicious and tell myself to stop worrying, but more craziness was in store the rest of his tenth-grade year.

Carl and I shared our concerns with Hayden and let him know we would enforce our rules with consequences. We asked him to sit and write his goals for his new year and think about where he wanted to end up after he graduated. He had a hard time following through with that request. He was a day-to-day thinker and never seemed to look to the future. We didn't realize at the time that his mind would wander, and thoughts of using a substance were the only thing on his mind, which he later described to us. Hayden was a happy kid; I rarely saw him get angry, and he agreed to comply with the rules. So, life moved on, but Hayden could not move away from the stuff that continued to get him into trouble, and his need for drugs slowly continued to get worse.

I began to notice money was missing from my wallet. At least I thought it seemed to be. It was beyond my thoughts to even think one of my kids could be taking it, so I assumed I was not remembering I used it. This went on for several weeks, until I began to feel like an idiot. I decided to start keeping tabs on how much I had before I went to bed every night. One day I realized I was missing another $20 bill. I approached each of the kids, and Hayden confessed he needed it for school and was buying supplies at the bookstore. I let Hayden know he always needed to ask me for permission to get money, then made sure all the kids knew my purse was off-limits without asking.

As time went on, however, I believed more money went missing, and then I was hiding my purse. Having to hide my purse made me feel ridiculous in my own home. As I began to find stuff in Hayden's room again, like more empty, clear plastic button bags with faint residue on them; cigar paper; eye drops; small silver packages with weird pictures and letters on them; and lighters, I knew this is what he needed the extra money for. His weekend allowance for "bowling money" or "movie money" was not enough to cover the cost for the legal and illegal drugs he was craving.

We found ourselves in denial that all of this was as serious as it was. Our sweet, funny boy had become part of a dark world. Like the dream, he had been "swallowed up" by something huge, and we began to realize that we didn't even know our own son. *Who is this person living in our house?* We began to ask ourselves, *How did this happen?* Our upper-class, white child was now dressing like a gangster/rapper, wearing big clothes, flat-bill hats, and jewelry. He was obsessed with rap music as well. He listened to it constantly and was known for his rapping ability around school. He could perform nonstop freestyle rap better than all of his friends. We would listen and were impressed at his ability to sing and rap at first but soon realized he was seeing himself doing that for a living. This was the music of the times and was becoming very popular, so our kid was not the only one dressing the part. Years later, he told me drugs also aided him in lyric-writing, and he was writing music and selling CDs to make extra money for his drugs. The many different drugs he began trying were changing him, and the worst was still to come.

He was harming his brain and delaying his brain maturation by smoking marijuana and taking others' prescription drugs, we later learned. Despite the daytime planners and extra tutors, he was becoming very disorganized and having trouble keeping up with his schoolwork. Hayden's grades continued to drop because all he could think about was how he would get drugs for the weekend, whom he would get them from, how he would pay for them, and where he would use them.

Some of his teachers at the high school called us in for a meeting to address situations that were occurring at school. He was falling behind and would skip a class here and there and make jokes out loud at school about drugs, which a few teachers heard. We were trying to understand and put the different scenarios together, that Hayden had some type of mental problem or was just turning into a bad kid. Nothing made sense yet, so we continued with punishment, stricter rules, and a doctor's visit to get a physical exam.

The next year and half was miserable and more frustrating than anything we had ever had to think about. Hayden was living for the weekend to come, and suffering within. We continued punishing him by keeping him home and taking his car or his cell phone away. We kept hoping he would pull himself together, but time after time the trust would be broken. Hayden began stealing from his brother and sisters and selling items from his own room to buy marijuana or pills from a kid who was dealing drugs at school. I had some very special golden rings that I couldn't find, but it didn't occur to me that he had taken them. During this time, his teachers were letting him repeat work to get his grades back up because we lived in a school district that was very competitive, and most students were striving for excellence. We felt embarrassed and knew he would have to be removed from class if his situation did not get better.

We then made the decision to take Hayden to a psychologist for testing to see if he had a learning disorder or other issues that kept him from thriving. The thought of him being an addict never crossed our minds, and by this point he was hiding his use better.

In my mind, addicts lived in the nasty streets and did not come from upscale families. Because my grandfather was an alcoholic, my parents led me to believe a certain stigma about addiction, that it is a choice and after many years of use, one might become addicted to the product they are using.

I also took Hayden to see our family doctor, who ran some quick tests and found out Hayden showed symptoms of ADHD, so he began medication and we enrolled him in a brain-sharpening program that cost us $3,000. A company convinced us that he needed to train his brain into better habits and that this would be great for him, so we were willing to try it, but three months into the program, the company went bankrupt. Hayden did not like the way the ADHD medication made him feel, and after a couple of months he refused to take it, and the brain games seemed to be doing nothing. I was then referred to a counselor so he could talk his issues out. We were unaware at the time, but he was also smoking marijuana on the weekends for the relaxed feeling, and this was conflicting with his ADHD medication. Marijuana stays in your system for up to three weeks and was counteracting his prescribed medication.

We decided it was time to start counseling in the middle of Hayden's junior year and thought a male counselor would be best. Hayden told us this was a waste of money, that he did not need a counselor, and he became agitated that he had to go. When it came time to leave for his appointment, he would not get in the car, and I spent time convincing him to. I was so frustrated but kept my cool for a better chance to get him in the car.

At this point, we were extremely frustrated and were becoming very angry with Hayden. After he'd spent several weeks with his new counselor, we were advised to send Hayden away for treatment to a wilderness program that could shape him up. He would be gone for at least sixty days in the cold mountains of Montana—and this would be in the middle of his junior year, so we knew he would not be able to graduate with his class. It was a hard decision, but we felt we had no choice. Hayden was already behind in school, and we could tell he did not have the focus to catch up. When we broke the news to Hayden about the wilderness program, he was very upset and begged us not to send him. He began throwing out all kinds of promises about getting himself together and how he could change. It was hard to say good-bye, but we believed it was for the best. The night before he was leaving for Montana, he left the house and was gone for several hours. He did not tell us where he was going. When he finally returned home, he was not doing well and we knew he left to go use a substance. We did not know what all he was using at this time, but we had a hard time getting him to leave his room the next morning. He was in a bad mental state, and his emotions seemed so cold as I hugged him goodbye. He was very disconnected and stared at the floor until we finally convinced him to get in the car. Carl flew with him to Montana and said his good-byes to Hayden, even though he was upset for being left there. Hayden was going to miss his drugs more than he missed us, sadly. We spent our first $30,000 at this rehab. We had high hopes of him returning clean and sober, ready to get on with life. We just knew our old, funny Hayden would return to us, and we could return to the plan we made for him.

We were allowed one visitation in the two months he was there. When we arrived, it was about fifteen degrees and the wind was blowing. I felt bad because Hayden hated cold weather, and he was miserable. Even though it was cold, it was beautiful. The property was sunk into a valley between mountains, and the smell of burning wood filled the air. Hayden was not able to see the beauty around him. The guys were spread out into large cabins in groups and slept on bunkbeds. Hayden was used to his comfortable bed in his own big room and the freedom to eat and watch TV whenever he wanted. This place was a huge change, and we knew change would make an impact. The residents would be awakened every morning by a counselor with a firm, loud voice and then taken to group therapy before daily chores.

To our surprise, halfway through Hayden's treatment, the wilderness counselors informed us that no addict should ever return to their original home. Did they say addict? Drug addict? We were told this was treatment for troubled teens, and he needed to learn self-discipline, which would control his behavior and drug use. They advised us to send Hayden to live in the boarding school up in that area, but we were his parents and we felt we should continue raising him ourselves. The thought of letting other people raise Hayden was not an option and did not fit into our plans. Instead of trusting his counselor, we decided Hayden would return home to us. Besides, we were led to believe from his previous therapist that he just needed to be "whipped" into shape and have a better attitude. We assumed he would be fine after following this sixty-day counseling program, which included firm talks from his supervisor, strong, enforced rules, as well as a trip into the freezing-cold mountains to learn how to follow rules and gain self-discipline.

All I could assume was that these wilderness counselors dealt more with behavioral issues and less with addiction from Hayden's outcome and lack of help. Because he did have trouble following those rules when hiking in the cold, he contracted frost bite on his toes and was miserable. After recovering from the frostbite, he was required to spend the night outside alone and had to bury himself in the ground to stay warm. Hayden had some self-discipline training and obstacle courses onsite that were supposed to help him gain self-confidence. After all of this, how could he not be able to follow rules, come home with a better attitude, and stop using drugs, which were making life so complicated for him? For the first time, someone was calling him a drug addict, and we were not convinced that our son was "one of them." We did not want to believe it and were in denial because we lacked education and understanding at the time, but he was an addict.

What we did notice was our son was now a cigarette smoker because that was allowed at the treatment center. Even though he was there to get better, he was now addicted to nicotine. We were not prepared for that at all and did not know they allowed the guys to smoke there, so now he was addicted to cigarettes. Hayden had been in the program a month and was very ready to come home, and we could tell he seemed depressed. Because we chose not to send him to a boarding school, the only other option they said we had was to sell our home and move to another location. They suggested that we move away from the area where he bought his drugs and away from his drug-using friends for the best success. It actually made sense to us that Hayden would have to come home with a fresh new start and find all new friends in a new area and attend a new school, but we eventually realized not even small, new towns were safe from easy drug access. We started researching online and processing Hayden's past behaviors and realized he was not just a bad kid with a bad attitude but that something more serious was going on in his head. It was hard to say at first, but Carl and I started to believe our son was an addict.

We called a family meeting to discuss this with our other three children, and graciously, they agreed that we should move to help Hayden. We had one month to find the right house, just as the Christmas holidays were rolling around. After searching for a few days, we came across the perfect find. A big, beautiful home on twelve acres in the up-and-coming small town of Fairview, Texas, about forty minutes north of Dallas; the schools were good and the people were friendly. The area was beautiful, with widespread farmland and open-range livestock grazing. This is where we would settle in before Hayden was even out of the wilderness program. We listed our home on the market, packed everything up, and quickly moved into our new house. The kids settled in just as the holidays were ending. It was a new beginning for all of us. If I had known then what I know now and what I've lived through, I would have enrolled Hayden into a boarding school and not brought him home.

The move came as a huge surprise to Hayden. We decided not to tell him until the day he departed from Montana. He finished his second month, and we made plans to fly him home. Carl made the flights with him again, explained the reasons for our move, and hoped he would embrace the idea quickly. When he arrived at our new home, we could sense the depression, and there was no sign of any spark in his eyes. He sat staring for a while on the big back porch as we talked with him and tried to help put it into perspective for him. We quickly enrolled him into school, in hopes to help him feel comfortable with our decision and get back to a normal life with a normal routine. The superintendent of the school district was wonderful and knew our situation. He wanted to help as much as possible and spent some time with Hayden, trying to mentor him and get him in the right classes at school. We felt a great deal of support and felt we had made the right choice to move to Fairview.

Because Hayden was very likeable, he made friends quickly, but emotionally, he seemed to struggle to feel right around people. He invited large groups over but didn't socialize much. It was like he was making an effort so we would believe he was doing well. We began looking for a counselor even though he told us he did not need one; he just needed some time to get used to the new area. He began to feel very anxious and nervous around large crowds. We thought everything would be better because of the two-month wilderness program, but it did not take long for Hayden to find two boys at the school who were secretly selling benzodiazepines and offered him Xanax pills.

We were not familiar with this substance at the time but quickly learned that Xanax was prescribed to patients with severe anxiety or trauma in their life and was prescribed for short term use because it was highly addictive. Many times, people would not finish medications and leave them on counters or in cabinets, and teens could take them themselves or sell them. Without us knowing, Hayden was already struggling with thoughts of drug use and relapse, so without much thought, he took two pills and placed them in a coat pocket.

He was trying to tell himself he didn't need them, but his consuming thoughts had only been suppressed in Montana, not helped. The rush he got out of just thinking of using was all it took to keep him trapped in the belly of the grotesque serpent as in my dream, still heading deeper into the unknown place, further away from me. When he arrived home that day, we talked, but he was hiding his feelings and left the Xanax in his coat pocket until morning, still trying not to use them. We later found out.

He arrived back at school and sat in his desk, trying to just get by until the bell rang and he could come home. Before the bell could ring, however, drug dogs were brought to visit the school that day, and they started in the school parking lot. The cigarettes Hayden had in his car on school campus were enough to alert the dogs and get him pulled from class. As Hayden approached the office, the campus police officer with a drug dog in hand noticed the dog's reaction toward Hayden, and the scene changed very quickly. The dogs alerted the officer of a substance present on Hayden. Before he could realize what was about to happen, the officers pulled the Xanax out of his pocket, and Hayden was handcuffed and quickly taken to jail. I received the call around 2 p.m., just before school let out, and was devastated. I could not believe what I was hearing. My son was taken to jail? He had gone away for two months was supposed to be fine! Who were these boys that did this to him and gave him the stuff? I was so angry. I called Carl immediately, and then we began to look for a lawyer. I was scared for Hayden to be in jail and so was he. Hayden spent the night there in a roomful of criminals, sleeping on the floor. We posted bond and got him out the next day, but this would not be the last time he would be behind bars.

When we were able to sit down with him, he convinced us that he made a stupid mistake by taking the pills from the kid at school and that he would not do that again. He would not tell us who had given him the pills because he was afraid it would look bad if he snitched. We believed him and wanted our new, happy life to continue, despite the fact that we had been informed that by Hayden having a controlled substance on school campus that was not prescribed to him, he now faced felony charges. We had moved to Collin County, one of the toughest counties in the nation on crime, and we had a battle ahead.

Because his car was on the school campus when he received a felony, the police asked for his car keys and took it to a holding lot; we never got that car back. We were confused about how they could keep our property, but supposedly, it was labeled as evidence. We believe it was a way for them to make money because eventually they could resell it. Our lawyer said we could continue to ask for it and might have a chance for its return to us but the car never did. A court date was set for Hayden, and we would have to wait for his verdict.

Due to the incident at school, Hayden would now be in school suspension and not allowed back on campus. He was placed in a portable building with a few other students who had caused trouble at school, and all of his work would be sent over to him, where he was on watch. He was starting to slowly regress as his disease was growing and getting stronger, pulling his thoughts into darkness again. Focusing on school became difficult as his mind was consumed with thoughts of using. He began using marijuana and prescription drugs once again, which

I discovered due to observing his strange behavior. He was getting to know the local dealers around town and was giving up on making new friends at school, even though he longed for friendship. He began trying to reconnect with old friends he had left behind in Highland Park, even though we told him he should not. Familiar items started showing up in Hayden's room, such as baggies and tiny plastic sacks, as well as lighters and empty wine bottles. We also searched his car and found eye drops and cough syrup bottles, such as Robitussin, which contains alcohol. Carl collected wine from unique vendors and displayed them in our wine cellar. He took pride in the collection and studied the regions the grapes were grown in. The collection was small but organized neatly in the cellar, just around the corner from our bedroom. I noticed, one day, a bottle was missing and asked Carl if he had taken one down. He said no, but I looked around for it and could not locate the missing bottle. A few days later, I was putting clothes away in Hayden's room and found the wine bottle empty. We began to realize that Hayden was stealing them and possibly drinking alone in his room. The collection began to shrink, and once we noticed what was happening, we had to hide them and keep them out of sight. New items were also showing up, and for the first time, I found a small, rainbow-colored glass item with a hole in the back and a hole on top. I smelled it and knew it was used to smoke marijuana. I also found pieces of burnt foil, burnt spoons, and several hollowed-out pens behind his bed and in his desk but had no idea what those items were being used for. I began to search on the internet for drug-related items, and all of these showed up on my screen to confirm he was now smoking black tar heroin. Our hearts were breaking because we now completely believed our son was an addict and would need to go to another rehab. His legal charges would complicate the matter, and we had to get several doctors and Hayden's psychiatrist to write letters agreeing that he desperately needed help with addiction issues. Our lawyer would take all this information into court to make a plea for Hayden so he could go for help before his trial. The appointed judge would need to believe Hayden was sick enough in order to make the decision to reschedule his court date. By some miracle, Hayden was able to finish up his junior year again; we got approval from the court judge to release him, and off he went to St. Jude's forty-five-day rehab in upstate New York. Their website looked promising, with a new approach in recovery from addiction. We had researched for hours trying to find the best one. St. Jude did not believe in the twelve-step approach but claimed recovery was more about clearing the mind and breaking bad habits. They assured us their way could turn him around in thirty to forty-five days. So we dished out another $18,000 in hopes that our son would return home well again. Sadly, we would face one of the hardest years to come after he returned.

—4—

Sex Offender

It was 2011 and Hayden was returning from his forty-five-day stay at St. Jude addiction recovery program. When he arrived home, he seemed in good spirits, and we hoped that the worst was behind us. He was required to be involved in another program upon return, so we put him in an outpatient addiction program for extra support that he attended several times a week. He was also back on probation and required to see his probation officer once a month for evaluation and drug-use screening. He was glad to be home and knew he needed to finish high school and graduate. He was trying to complete his senior year, so we enrolled him online with Texas Tech's high-school program instead of a local school. He turned eighteen during the summer, so he worked hard to accomplish all he needed to, but it was a struggle for him. Emotionally, he did not feel good about himself and was dealing with feelings of anxiety and depression. He had lost contact with most of his new friends, made no contact with any old ones, and for him to have no friends was a very lonely time. We encouraged him to go to church and get involved with the singles' group, but even though he said that was a good idea, he never came with us.

Our oldest daughter, Miranda, was close to Hayden and was so glad he had returned home. Growing up, Miranda looked up to Hayden and loved his funny jokes. They would spend time listening to music and watching scary movies with Landon. We would all gather at night to sing and say a prayer before bedtime. Sometimes Hayden would help Miranda with schoolwork and take time to listen to her. Miranda loved her brother dearly and knew he would always be there for her. It was hard for her to understand what was going on with Hayden. She knew we kept sending him away for help, and, like us, every time he returned, she believed everything was going to be okay.

Because we were new to our area, Miranda was trying to find good friendships, which had been a slow process. She was trying to get to know other people but realized doing so could be difficult in middle school, and she felt left out. At the end of her eighth-grade year, however, she made a new friend and was very happy. A girl named Katelyn started to notice Miranda at school and quickly befriended her. Miranda was a sweet, beautiful girl and had turned fourteen. She was blond and blue-eyed with great facial features and a cute figure. I called her my little Barbie doll. She loved to dress cute and had a passion for shoes and was already talking about being a fashion designer someday. She was a little on the shy side but was full of energy and longing for friendship. They became close friends, and Katelyn began spending a lot of time at our house during the summer. Katelyn was a pretty girl with brown hair and hazel eyes, and she was a few months older than Miranda but also fourteen. Her dad was a preacher who was trying to help establish a new church, and her mom was friendly. They had an older daughter who had run off a few years before with her Turkish boyfriend, and they were still bitter about the situation, even though she had returned home. In the past, they had also had some trouble with Katelyn that we were unaware of and found out too late from other parents. These parents later told me they did not know me well enough and felt uncomfortable talking about the family, but they felt bad after our situation occurred. So we opened our home to

Miranda's new friend, and they began spending much time together. Miranda was feeling better about the move and was so glad to have a close friend. The girls would come downstairs to eat dinner or watch TV, and on occasion, Hayden would be there when he was not working the part-time job he got himself or attending outpatient support groups. We believed he was doing well, and he was about to graduate online high school. He was coming and going out of the house and at times coming in late. Sadly, he was relapsing and beginning to use drugs again. He would begin to thirst for that feeling of relief.

We shared Hayden's struggles with Katelyn's family because we were getting to know them, and they were praying for him and hoped he would get better. They knew he had been in rehab and was now home, and so did Katelyn. I began to notice her watching Hayden when he would come through the kitchen on his way to his room. A few times, I found Miranda and her in his room listening to music, which became concerning because Hayden was a good-looking kid and I could tell Katelyn enjoyed seeing him. I talked with the girls and then Hayden and said being in his room was not allowed. I felt a responsibility to Katelyn's parents, and I knew it would concern them if their daughter was hanging out in his room because he was recently back from drug rehab. Miranda was confused about why they could not be in there, but I said it was better for everyone. Hayden had been home a few months and school started back up. Days passed and weekends came and went, but Katelyn continued to encourage Miranda to let her come over most weekends. She seemed to be controlling the situation, but Miranda did not want to lose her friend, so Katelyn called all the shots. Something just did not feel right. I didn't want to seem judgmental, so I decided to give their relationship more time. Miranda's emotions were still fragile from Hayden's situation coming and going to rehab, so I put my thoughts aside and will forever regret letting them stay friends.

Katelyn began struggling at school and not doing well at home. She had become obsessed with Hayden and was spending time with him that we were unaware of. Her sleepovers with Miranda were turning into sleepovers with Hayden. We didn't know it at the time, but Hayden had begun relapsing by experimenting with new drugs and coming home high on substances, and she would lie in his bed and wait for him to get home. This had been going on for months, and I felt like an idiot that I did not notice it. Hayden was glad someone was noticing him and did not think of any consequences; he was not feeling as lonely now. Soon, Hayden and Katelyn became a "couple." She wanted Hayden to have a Facebook account, so she put one together for him. He was not into social media at the time, but she showed him how to set up an account, use it, and begin establishing his friendships. Hayden wasn't maturing for his age because his substance abuse had delayed his thinking ability and information-processing skills. His psychiatrist informed us that he felt Hayden had the mind of a fourteen- or fifteen-year-old and that was why he was having such a hard time graduating and completing his senior year. Drugs delayed brain maturity and combinations of substances were even worse, which caused impairment and poor judgment. Miranda was destroyed inside when she came to an understanding of how involved her brother and best friend had become. She began to notice Katelyn leaving the room late at night and was eventually told they were a couple. She was too scared to say anything and just went along with all of it. Deep down, she was feeling used, and Katelyn was encouraging her to do things she knew she should not. Miranda began to struggle with depression and not feeling well. She was missing school and contracted mono. It was wearing her down to keep all of the secrets. After several months, Katelyn started to brag about her relationship, and other friends were becoming aware of the situation. At five months of seeing each other, a kid finally told Katelyn's parents what she knew about the relationship between Hayden and Katelyn. Her parents were concerned about her dropping grades at school and the lack of motivation that she had developed, but when they heard the news of her relationship with Hayden, they were outraged and completely shocked. They felt a drug addict had seduced their precious daughter. Late that evening, they had Katelyn message Hayden through the Facebook account she had set up and ask him to come pick her up at her home. Hayden left our house, not realizing he was going into a trap. Her family had called the police so they could hide down the dark street and wait to bust Hayden. As he arrived and pulled up to get Katelyn, lights began flashing, and he was immediately handcuffed, arrested, and taken in to face sex offender charges. He was horrified and let them take him away, off to jail. That call we received from him that night was like a knife in our hearts. We felt absolute devastation as he began telling us the details. Now he was not only a drug addict and a felon but labeled a sex offender. He was eighteen, and she was fourteen. He took all the punishment, and she walked away and got to start at a new school. We were against the relationship and knew it should not have happened, but when Hayden and Miranda told me the same story and did not have any chance of communicating about it, I knew it was true. I was very sorry for the situation but outraged by the way her parents had handled it. We felt all the bottled-up anger they had from the past had caused them to "explode" in the present and not think twice about the impact on anyone else. We assumed Katelyn's story was not the complete truth when she talked to her mom and dad. I made one last cell-phone call to her mother to enlighten her about her daughter's behavior—that she was not innocent like they assumed she was. Miranda was being influenced and encouraged by Katelyn to sleep with boys. She also bragged about how Hayden was not the first boy she had slept with. Her mother was in denial and told me never to call again. I said I did not need to because she knew the truth now.

Carl attended the court hearing a few weeks later because I was too emotional. They charged Hayden with a felony of online solicitation of a minor. The Facebook account Katelyn set up for him was now being used to hang him. Within the next two weeks, we would have to go in to hear what his limitations were and what he would be expected to do as a sex offender. Hayden spent three months in jail for the first part of his punishment and was a little nervous because this would be the longest time he had spent locked up. In the past, he had only spent a few days before we posted bond to get him out. He turned himself in to jail to start his sentence. Carl and I took turns visiting Hayden, and we set things up so his counselor was given visitation rights. Hayden's lawyer also saw him on occasion, and we were all trying to help keep his spirits up. While incarcerated, he was volunteering and able to work in the laundry room. The first week was hard, coming off of the drugs he was using, but we knew he was forced to stay clean while he was in there, and that seemed to be the only benefit. He attended church service when they offered it and enjoyed the music. A few weeks after being there, it was time to move him to a new cell with a new cell mate. They constantly moved inmates around to fit everyone new in and to send off the old inmates. To make matters worse, he was put in a cell with a gang member who had been a violent offender in the past, and he was a returning criminal. Hayden, being Hayden, was trying to befriend the guy and would make conversation with him in hopes of keeping the peace. Hayden would share information with us at visitation and was giving his new cell mate the benefit of the doubt. As time passed, his mate began to be demanding and started bullying Hayden. He named Hayden his bitch and demanded the food Hayden brought down from the vendor window be given to him. We had set up an account with funds Hayden could use to get snacks and toiletries to keep in his cell and use as needed. Inmates with family involvement usually had these accounts set up for them by family members because the cafeteria gave the inmates very limited food amounts. As Hayden refused to give up his food, he turned to look at his cell mate and received a fist to his face. The guy punched him out of anger, and Hayden was stunned but quickly pushed the emergency button there in the closed cell, which is used to alert guards of a problem. The emergency alarm sounded and guards quickly arrived. Hayden was removed from the cell and taken to the doctor for an ice pack and examination. He sat in pain, holding ice on his face and waiting for his X-ray. The doctor finally x-rayed to see a fracture in Hayden's jaw and bone bruising. As the hours passed, his face became bruised and swollen, which made him very uncomfortable, so he was given only Tylenol and not any opioids because his file had disclosed that he was an addict. That evening, he called to tell us the news about his injury, and we were shocked and angry. He spoke softly because it hurt to move his mouth.

A few days later, when I saw him through the visitation glass for the first time, I could not hold back the tears. I cried for a few minutes as Hayden sat quietly on the other side, still visibly shaken with tears in his eyes. I felt so helpless as I sat there, only getting to view my boy through the thick glass, and tried to say some encouraging words and understand how this could have happened. He explained the incident again, and I could see uncertainty in his eyes as he looked around while he talked. I wanted to hug him and didn't want to leave, but our time was up. We said our good-byes and hung up the communication phones. I could barely walk out of there, and my stomach was in a tight knot. There was not much we could do because there was no clear evidence about how the incident really happened, and the gang member was being moved to state prison anyway. Our lawyer told us it was better if we did not press charges because the guy was part of a gang. We thought about the rest of the family and decided not to risk it. It was hard to let it go, and I struggled for weeks.

Hayden healed and finished his three months in jail. Upon release, I picked him up and took him to see his court-appointed processor who would process all of Hayden's paperwork and explain the intense program that Hayden would be on for many years as a registered sex offender. She took the three of us into a small, closed room there at the courthouse. She spoke softly, and one by one, she began to list everything and every place Hayden would never be able to go again. He could not go to parks, schools, swimming pools, libraries, fast-food places with playgrounds, jobs where children would be, malls, bookstores, bathrooms a kid might use, and could not live within a hundred feet of a school, nursery, or church with a nursery.

My head was spinning from anxiety; I could not hold back the tears, and I watched as Hayden did not really seem to process how much more difficult life was about to become. The woman also began to explain the sex-offender class Hayden would have to attend once a week that involved one-on-one therapy and group discussion. Even though he was a teen, he was still put in a class with older men who were registered sex offenders as well. No matter what the age or type of charge, everyone attended the same groups. The woman knew all of the information was hard to hear, and she kept asking if we were okay so she could continue reading the rules. To our surprise, Hayden would be fitted with a permanent GPS monitor that needed to be worn at all times. He was referred to the county monitoring system to be fitted with a large black box and heavy-duty black strap to be worn around his ankle.

We finished up and she gave him his folder with many pages of instructions. Hayden's sex-offender meetings started the next week, and he would come in at night, sick to his stomach after listening to men talk for hours and answer questions about what they had done to small children. He had nothing in common with them and came in angry that he had to be in the group. His mistake was nothing like theirs, and even his group therapist recognized it and would talk to Hayden after groups. I tried to have him moved into a private-counseling setting instead, but his probation officer would not grant that to him and said the judge would not grant it either.

We began living on edge day after day that Hayden would mess up somehow and be in the wrong place at the wrong time. He was so nervous about where he went and afraid a kid would be in his area and they would throw him back in jail. Week after week, each offender group meeting made him come home upset. He told me very little about what he had to listen to and was obviously bothered by it. Carl and I would talk with our lawyer but not receive much help.

Weeks passed, and the stress was so great that Hayden would sweat if we went out and would constantly look around. He would tell me how nervous he felt, so I made sure he continued to see a psychiatrist in addition to all his other meetings. He could not stay clean, however, and began to use drugs to escape reality, which impacted his ability to take care of his responsibilities. I was trying to manage all of his probation meetings, community volunteering, and get him to his sex-offender meetings because I knew they would throw him back in jail if he missed any of his assignments. He lost interest in taking care of himself and said his heart was beating hard at times. He began to feel unwell, so I took him to our primary-care doctor, who diagnosed him with high blood pressure. He was given medication to reduce it, but I knew this would be another area where I would have to monitor his situation to be sure he was taking the medication.

Hayden began to relapse and was consumed with thoughts of using to ease all of the discomfort, which became apparent as time went on. He had been to several counselors and a psychiatrist but never completely opened up to them and was in denial about how sick he really was. He did not call himself an addict and did not want to talk about it. One morning, he was headed to a follow-up appointment with a doctor and he had used drugs the night before and then taken his blood-pressure medication early that morning. He left the house at nine that morning—about the time I had some painters working on our home. They had seen Hayden in the kitchen and watched him drive away just before they left to get some paint supplies. About five minutes after they left, I got a phone call from them asking about Hayden's car's make and model. They believed he was the reason for the huge line holding up traffic and possibly in a wreck ahead. I quickly grabbed my purse, called Hayden, and headed down the road. We lived out on twelve acres, but we were near several neighborhoods and a new fire station, which bordered a busy street taking people to and from the highway. Within a couple of minutes, I was at the back of a long line, and Hayden was not answering his cell phone. I pulled over onto a driveway to get my car off the road. I was too far back to see what was going on down at the bottom of the hill, so I began to run down the sidewalk toward the situation. As I got closer, I could see lights flashing and hear people talking. Upon approaching the scene, I discovered the front of a smashed white work van, and a large man being removed from behind the wheel, which had been thrust into his chest. I could see Hayden's black car completely totaled in the front, with his engine exposed and two firemen working to free him from the tangled mess. His foot was lodged under the brake, and he was very shaken up but alive. He too had hit the steering wheel, and, for some reason that day, he remembered to put on his seat belt. He and I had argued a lot about him wearing a seat belt but he usually didn't. If I was driving and he hadn't put his on, I would sit and wait until he did. The belt saved his life that day. He had fallen asleep at the wheel just a few minutes after leaving the house because of the drug use and blood-pressure medication. We later found out his medication was too strong for him and put him to sleep.

I was in tears as I watched the paramedics put Hayden on a stretcher and load him into the back of the ambulance, but I was glad he was alive. He had a fractured foot and many bruises, but he was released the next day. He hobbled around on crutches for about a week, which made it harder for him to get his fix, but he still managed to have a "friend" supply him, he later told us. He would text a dealer he had been in contact with previously and ask him to come down the road we lived on and meet him in the driveway. At times, the other kids and I would be at home and Hayden would say a friend from outpatient stopped by to say hello. Addicts do not think about the risks they put others in to get what they feel they cannot live without. Some time passed and we began to notice the same changes in his attitude, and I began finding clues in his room that he was relapsing, and relapsing hard by the looks of his room and his secretive nature. His foot healed, but he became pretty messed up and was starting to stay closed up in his room. When he did eventually come out, Carl or I would fight with him. The other kids could hear the foul language Hayden was starting to use and the anger in his voice. Olivia and Miranda would shut their doors and try not to listen. Landon would leave the house to get away from it all.

We had been encouraged by other parents to kick Hayden out of the house, but with all of his charges, we knew he would spend many years in prison if he missed any of his meetings or failed a drug test. We loved him very much despite all of the trouble and wanted him to get well, therefore it was time to search for another rehab, and with our lawyer's help, we begged the courts to let him get the help he needed and put his charges and probation on hold for a second time. We took Hayden into court, and he looked terrible. He could barely answer questions, and we held our breath until word came that he had been granted a temporary hold on all charges so he could get the help he needed. We now believed he had to be somewhere much longer for more help, with a specialist involved. After more research, we felt relieved. We found a facility only forty-five minutes north of us in the country. A rehab center had been established just outside the small town of Van Alstyne called Enterhealth. It had everything from typical group meetings to brain rehab and meditation. A doctor was on-site as well to manage medications and withdrawals and a psychiatrist was on-site for one-on-one counseling, so we were hopeful and glad to see all of the help they could offer. Just because they offered it, though, didn't mean everyone would accept it. But we had high hopes that Hayden would.

When the day came for us to get Hayden settled into the Enterhealth Ranch addiction treatment center, he didn't want to go. Carl and I spent an hour reminding him what would happen to him if he stayed. It was very hard to reason with him when he was using. We finally got him in the car and hoped the transition would be smooth once we got him there. We all toured the place, and Hayden met the staff and doctors. We had a family meeting and ate lunch there before we left for home. He spent the first several days going through withdrawals and being sick. The next four months he lived there, he seemed to be making great progress. He still had his stubborn streaks and stayed disorganized with chores, however, and his counselor could see he was immature for his age and had her concerns. After testing and counseling him, she believed he had borderline personality disorder because he seemed uncomfortable in his own skin and obsessed with wearing rapper-type clothes. He watched videos and listened to rap music much of the time, trying to identify with a culture opposite of the one he was growing up in. He seemed to be obsessed with the way rappers dressed and what they sang about. It was hard to understand because we had established a good life for him. His wardrobe consisted of very oversized jeans, large emblemed T-shirts, flat-billed hats, and a gold chain. We tried for so long to get him to wear other apparel, but he refused and felt comfortable in that style, but they would not let him wear his hat and chain there. We were glad and supported that decision.

Despite his issues, he was very likeable and polite when he was there. As he became sober, he always returned to the Hayden we knew and was easier to talk with. He would find his humor again and was liked by the staff and other patients. We attended parent support groups and tried to make the best of our visits, learning as much as we could to understand our son's disease. While he was at Enterhealth for his treatment, the damage left behind on our other kids was apparent. We spent time talking with each of them to keep everyone involved with the family and have some kind of understanding about what disease Hayden was living with. We were open and honest and hoped to have some healing time while he was away.

Enterhealth was the first coed treatment center Hayden attended because in the past he went to rehab with guys only. Everyone there was instructed not to get attached to any other resident and strictly focus on recovery. Clear instructions were made that upon departure, no one of the opposite sex should stay in contact with each other. Statistics showed the chance of staying clean was better for those who followed those rules. As chance would have it, Hayden connected well with one girl there, and they became friends quickly. She was a year older then him but was also struggling with drug addiction. They both heard the rules but didn't believe never talking again made sense and wanted to stay friends. Hayden casually mentioned to us what the exit rules were, so we agreed he should follow them. It only took a few days after being released from Enterhealth, however, when the calls between them began.

—5—

Cuts

The spring Hayden was arrested on sex-offense charges was a very difficult one for all of us. In the past, I heard about cases like Hayden's and how difficult it was for a teen to receive these charges, but it never even crossed my mind that one of my own ever would. The thought of a sex offender being near my own girls made me cringe from sad stories I had heard, and I knew my son was not one of them. I did not want Olivia to hear this information about Hayden because she was so young; I felt there was no purpose in sharing any of it with her. She was aware something very sad happened, so I kept it as simple as possible and let her know Hayden made a mistake and was still sick. I often wondered who knew our situation and hoped it would not impact her. I was volunteering at the kids' schools, meeting new people and making friends, hoping people would see we were a good family and helping reduce the negative feelings they might have about Hayden. It was a smaller town, and people talked, so my goal was to be sure the other three kids were not impacted greatly because of misunderstandings about our situation with Hayden's problems.

During these tough years, Olivia was my little sunshine, and when I was feeling down, sad, hurt, or scared, her smile would bring me joy. I would spend time with her, which reminded me of Hayden when he was young and disease-free and, oh, how I wished everything could be different for him. I felt we were living two lives because of age differences and circumstances. We had the life with Hayden in it, which seemed to bring a sad darkness time and time again, every time he relapsed, and the one without him for the family's sake when he was at rehab. I did, however, continue to stay positive and was trying to be a good mom to bring peace to the family. Carl and I found time for each other and always kept the communication lines open. We made sure we listened to each other and worked together to keep the family bond strong. By this point, we had both sides of our family praying for us and sending words of encouragement.

Miranda was so torn inside and felt a tremendous amount of guilt that she had never said anything about her best friend and her brother's relationship. She did not want to lose her friend or see her brother be sent away again. She began to get sick and miss school, and she started telling me she was depressed and very sad. She would lie on the floor and cover her face, not wanting to get up. One evening, Miranda confided in me and explained everything that she had lived through and felt she had to hide the past five months. As I sat there listening, my heart began to break. I felt like a failure. How had I missed so much? All I ever wanted to be was a wonderful mom and had given so much time and energy to the family. It was now one battle after another. I began to feel I wasn't doing enough to protect my kids and wished I had not been naive.

I assured Miranda we understood and did not want her to feel guilt. She was put in a tough spot and did make a mistake by not telling us, but she needed to forgive herself, and we, too, forgave her. She held on to her feelings and wanted a sense of control over a situation she could not control. Miranda did not know how to handle what she was feeling because she was depressed and angry at the same time. She could not undo the damage. Her heart was hurting, and she wanted some relief.

A few mornings later, I went upstairs to wake her for school and walked over to her bed to give her a kiss on the forehead. As she began to move around to wake up, I noticed a red slash on the inside of her arm a few inches above her wrist. Her long sleeve had slid up her arm to expose the cut. I said, "Goodness, when did this happen?"

Her eyes opened as I reached to gently touch the cut, and she pulled her shirt over it. She said she accidently scraped herself, and that was the explanation I needed. It did not cross my mind that it was anything other than an accident. A few days passed and another morning arrived to make sure Miranda was up and getting ready for school. She was supposed to be setting an alarm to wake herself but wasn't. I went into her room, and she was asleep on her back with her forearm exposed and several more cuts near the other one that had started healing. I stood there staring for a minute to get a better look before waking her. I didn't know what to think about the marks on her arm and stood in silence for a minute to process what I was seeing. The only time I had seen the issue of someone cutting themself was in the movie *28 Days* with Sandra Bullock. It was a movie about addiction, and one girl in the movie was known for cutting her arms. I did not know anyone personally and had no understanding of this issue whatsoever. I knew people slit their wrists to commit suicide, which gave this situation a sense of urgency. I was very confused.

I woke Miranda gently and spoke to her calmly. "Honey, I see you have more slashes on your arm in the same place. Can you please tell me what is happening?"

She turned away from me and did not want to talk.

My heart picked up its pace and I asked if she was doing this to herself. A few seconds passed and I asked again, trying to stay calm.

She slowly answered, saying yes while keeping her eyes shut not to look at me. I sat down on her bed in silence because I did not know what to say and did not know what this meant. I had no understanding of this behavior at all. She could not explain it to me but did tell me she used scissors to do it. I walked into her bathroom and could see a few small tissues with blood on them in her trash can. She had school to get ready for, so I told her we would talk later in the day. She wore a long-sleeved shirt to school to hide the wounds, and I put on a smile to hide mine.

Olivia needed help getting ready and breakfast had to be made, so I pulled myself out of shock-mode and into mom-mode. Landon came down to eat and headed out the door, and then the bus arrived for Olivia. I dropped Miranda off at school and wished her a good day. I was fighting the tears, and my heart felt her cuts. Something was wrong, and I knew she needed help.

Carl and I talked, and he was just as confused as I was about this new situation we found ourselves in. He said to get her a counselor for some help. After I went upstairs to Miranda's room to remove the scissors from her bathroom, I spent several hours looking online for the right person to help us and came across a website that was titled A Safe Place to Heal. It was a counseling group, and I felt it might be the right one, so I made a call and left a message. About an hour later, I received a call back from a sweet voice on the other end, and she wanted to hear what our situation was. After I explained some details, she said, "I want her to see Tricia. I believe this will be a good fit for her and you." I graciously said thank-you, and we set a meeting for two days later.

School ended for the day. I picked up Miranda, and she seemed fine. We talked about her day on the way home from school, and she said she was ready for the weekend. She always worked hard to keep her grades up and looked forward to getting out of high school to move on to college. Later in the evening, we discussed why she was cutting herself. She was glad that I'd found someone she could talk to who could help her other than Carl and me. She did not want to feel depressed like she had been for months now. She knew how concerned we were but had a hard time explaining what was going on in her head. She just said, "Somehow it makes me feel better when I'm done cutting myself."

Those words were very hard to hear because it sounded so bizarre. We did not want the other kids to know the damage she was doing to herself, so we did not talk of it for a while.

I was glad the day arrived to go to A Safe Place to Heal and meet Tricia. When we arrived, we waited a few minutes in the front office for her to get organized, and she came out and said she wanted to talk with Miranda alone first. After about forty-five minutes, she called me back so the three of us could talk. Tricia really wanted to help us, and Miranda agreed to come back. Before we left, Tricia explained what she knew about cutting and self-harm.

Surprisingly, she said that Miranda did not want to die but wanted to be in control. So much had happened in her life lately and she was hurting inside and wanted to be more in control of situations where she simply couldn't be. She'd been holding so much in for months because she did not know how to handle what she knew was wrong. When Tricia spoke, everything began to make sense, and I felt this would be a good place for Miranda. She explained the techniques she would use to help Miranda and the type of meetings we could expect. Miranda would have to be open and honest with her and us to get better. I could tell Miranda was at ease while we were there, so we set up the next several meetings. Carl and I would have to have patience and be very supportive of her. When we arrived home, Miranda was in a better mood and went upstairs to do homework. I made dinner and checked on the other kids. Carl would be getting in from work, so I spent time on the internet reading about cutting and trying to understand this mental state better.

During all of the struggles with Miranda, I was still trying to help Hayden manage his outpatient, twelve-step rehab meetings, sex-offender meetings, probation responsibilities, and volunteer work he was required to do. His schedule was so full, he didn't have time to work a real job. To occupy his mind in the available time he did have, he would write lyrics and make music on his Ableton Push music board that connected to his computer and looked like a music recording studio. He spent hours in his room making beats and sounds, which he would sing and rap to. We had our good days and our bad days, and Hayden was trying to keep his spirits up among all of the self-maintenance he needed. Something inside his head began to stir and convince him he needed to use for relief. His downward spiral began again a few months into Miranda's therapy for depression and cutting.

The meetings with Tricia were going well, even though Miranda was still cutting on occasion. Other incidents with people at school and mean words on Facebook caused her to cut as well. Besides talking with Tricia, the education I was giving myself from research was helping me deal with Miranda. I realized I could not fix her myself and hide every possible cutting utensil to keep her safe. She would have to work through this with our support and gain strength to stop on her own. Cutting actually became a casual conversation with Miranda, and I did not hesitate to talk about it. Tricia was able to get her to open up and discuss everything she was feeling. I was allowed to also attend some of the meetings, and Miranda realized I was able to deal with it and that her dad and I loved her very much regardless of the past. She began to get better, and we were seeing great progress.

One evening, however, just about 11 p.m. after everyone had gone to bed, Miranda was still up and angry about a text she received from someone at school. She thought about what was being said to her and realized she was not in control of the situation. Even though weeks had passed with no feelings to cut, something about this message got to her and she reached for the scissors in her desk. The old wounds were healing and recovering between the many marks she had made, but in her anger, she opened the scissors wide and pressed down much harder than she realized, just below the other cuts and closer to her left wrist. Blood came pouring out, and she was terrified and in shock. Loud, thundering footsteps came running down the stairs next to our room. She was crying and quickly came around the corner to wake us. Carl reached for his lamp, and as I sat up, I could see blood rushing down into her hand. Carl and I leapt out of bed, and I grabbed a towel while he sat her down because she looked pale and faintly. I wrapped a towel tightly around her arm, Carl scooped her up in his arms, and we raced for the car to get her to the emergency room. She lay in my lap as Carl drove us to the hospital, and I looked down at my beautiful girl and held back the tears. How could my child do this to herself? We'd been making such progress.

As we arrived, they rushed her into a room as we filled out paperwork. She needed thirteen stitches to close up the deep wound that would be held in place by an arm brace. She was given pain medication and was resting quietly when we were able to see her. We hugged her, and she knew she'd really scared us. I could tell she was still thinking about what had happened. The hospital's policy was to call Child Protective Services in when a minor is brought in with afflictions. When we found out this service had arrived and would first talk with Miranda alone, we were surprised. Carl and I sat in the waiting room, looking at each other, and agreed this situation was one we never imagined. Miranda reassured the agent that we were good parents and she was not suicidal but just struggling with some issues.

A psychiatrist on-call came in next to make sure Miranda was telling the truth and to evaluate her. I remember thinking, *They don't know that we love all of our children dearly, and we are doing everything in our power to keep them healthy. We go to church and we pay our bills. We have worked hard all our lives; we are good people.* I really wanted to yell it out loud, but I knew that would not help anything. We stayed calm, and Miranda was released to us after we answered many questions about her situation. We arrived back home around 3:00 a.m. that morning, and Miranda stayed home from school to rest. I could not sleep that night and lay wondering where we would go from there and what more we could do to help her. I thought Miranda was healing, but this new incident had me confused. I said a prayer and asked God for strength to face another day.

I set up a quick meeting to see Tricia the next day and let Miranda talk out her feelings and explain what had occurred. She was in pain for several days from the large cut on her arm that was trying to heal, but she was able to talk about it.

Weeks passed, and she went back to school, and we began seeing Tricia twice a week. Hayden and Landon were aware now that Miranda had been cutting herself but were very confused by the news. They knew she was getting help and didn't talk to her much about it. Olivia did see the bandage on Miranda's arm and knew she had hurt herself but was not told the details because I felt we needed to wait longer before trying to explain it to her. Miranda's schoolmates had seen her arm in the past and knew she was cutting herself, which gave her a stigma that limited her friendships. Miranda had her boyfriend as well as one friend who continued to stick by her side during all of this craziness. That was the last time Miranda ever cut herself. The shock and all of the blood sent a strong message to her brain, and, for the first time, she realized her cutting was in control of her. She came to believe and understand that to be in control meant she would not harm herself anymore. After a year of counseling, she found peace through the sessions we continued with Tricia and the openness Carl and I were able to provide. Our relationship grew strong, and she realized our love was unconditional.

Ninth grade ended, and the summer passed as well. Miranda was dreading going back to the same high school for tenth grade and wanted to be homeschooled. We wanted to support her as much as we could, so we found a private school that was very small and also online. It was a thirty-minute drive one way, so time management and balancing out everyone else's schedules became essential. Olivia started volleyball through the local city program that she had signed up for with some friends and now had practice and games every week in addition to school. Landon was in and out of the house between school and friends. Carl's work was going well, and we were both relieved that the family was also starting to seem well.

We and our extended family were praying for strength and peace. My parents had been torn up over all of the sad news we had begun sharing with them. They gave so much of their time to the kids when they were growing up and loved them deeply. We kept the information of Hayden's drug use to ourselves for the first couple of years but knew we could no longer hide it because of the impact it was causing the family. I remember trying to explain everything to my mom and hearing her distress and concern for us. It was hard for her and my dad to comprehend everything I was saying. Trying to explain everything else from Hayden's sex-offense charge to Miranda's cutting was very difficult. I still felt guilt and embarrassment that I had missed the clues that Hayden and Katelyn were seeing each other for so long. I prayed for God to forgive me and to help us heal. I had so much hatred in my heart for Katelyn and her family because of the choices they had made to press charges. I had to realize they were in denial about their daughter and her problems so I could one day forgive them and forgive myself for the terrible situation.

Fall was halfway over, and Miranda settled into her new school with a new routine. She was able to work from home and attend school as needed to meet with teachers and take tests. She was a smart girl, and I knew if this was her choice, she would succeed. She had goals set for herself and was determined to reach them. Watching her mature and gain her confidence back was refreshing. She was sad that Hayden had relapsed and had been sent to another rehab, but she was always hopeful that he would come back well. She still felt a little responsible for his new felony charge and believed his relapse was because of the pressure he was under from the sex-offense charge. As time passed, she was able to deal with her choices because of Tricia's counseling, and during our counseling sessions, she mentioned several times that she should have told me what she knew. We had to look forward and not look back, I would tell her. We could not fix the past, but we could try very hard to have a wonderful future by making good choices. She and I agreed to always talk out any issues that might arise. Carl and I knew it was important that our kids feel comfortable enough to discuss anything because every day seemed to be a learning experience. We kept our spirits up and prayed for guidance.

The holidays were fast approaching, and we were looking forward to family coming into town to celebrate with us. We were all going to miss Hayden again this year because he was away for treatment. He loved the holidays and being with family when he was well, so we hoped that maybe the next year, he could be included in the gathering.

—6—

Unlikely Felon

A new year arrived, and we were grateful that life seemed to calm down. Olivia was happy and doing well while we tried to keep her childhood as normal as possible. She loved her friends and had company to play as much as she could. School was a breeze, and she loved working on assigned projects. She was my ray of sunshine and brought light to the darkness. Miranda and I were still attending sessions with Tricia, and our bond was strong again. She was moving through her new online/private school well. We spent many hours in the car together, driving to and from the location, so we talked and laughed a great deal until she got her license. I was glad we listened to Miranda's needs and got her some support. I could see a maturity about her, and she was feeling happy again.

Hayden was home from Enterhealth, he was sober, and he was attending Narcotics Anonymous meetings for support. The kids were glad to have him home because he was his old, funny self again. Against our wishes, however, Hayden was dating Natalie from rehab. We wanted him to follow the advice from his last rehab and not date anyone he had been in treatment with. Natalie was a sweet girl and was living with her aunt and uncle in Dallas, about forty minutes away. The commute to see each other was a long one in traffic, but they began making the trip back and forth to either our house or her aunt's house. Hayden was back in a routine of probation meetings and sex-offender classes, which he hated. He became frustrated as the weeks passed and wondered how much longer he would be required to go to these meetings with older men and hear the horrific stories about what they had done.

Natalie knew his situation and was being supportive. She was struggling to get her life together, trying to work and get back in school. As the weeks passed, Hayden believed he could smoke a little marijuana to help him relax, which went completely against everything he had been in therapy/addiction recovery for. He brought some marijuana home and asked Landon to "chill" with him one evening out in the barn. Landon was glad to have some time with his big brother, so he jumped at the chance, but, while out there, Hayden lit up a joint and offered it to Landon. Some of Landon's friends also began smoking marijuana, so against his better judgment, he began to experiment with it.

For the most part, Landon kept a low profile and went with the flow of the family. He was always the quiet one growing up and had a kind mannerism about him. He was less likely to socialize and spent much time on computers and loved to build and create mechanical objects. Landon would fascinate us by his ability to build robots, potato shooters, and other objects. He enjoyed the twelve acres we were living on and drove around the land in "Big Red," the Honda utility vehicle, to find new projects and shoot guns. He was a good kid, and we had never had trouble with him. He kept his room clean and organized and enjoyed collecting football cards and memorabilia. He kept his grades up, even though it was hard to pay attention in class, and had a bright future ahead, as he was planning to become an engineer. He wanted to attend a four-year college after high school, so during his junior year, he and Carl took a trip to tour the University of Alabama and attended a football game. We started to help him look at what colleges he wanted to apply to. He gave up his football career plans and took up mixed martial arts twice a week. I would stay at the gym where he was training and watch him wrestle. It was obvious he was strong because as a beginner, he was doing well. At six-one, he was an asset when it came to pinning down his opponent.

When Landon and Hayden were young, Landon followed his big brother everywhere, and they spent much time together. Hayden was the typical big brother and picked on Landon, but I knew it was a matter of time before Landon outgrew Hayden and all of that would change. As they got older, Hayden became more aggressive and would sometimes talk tough to Landon. It seemed to be the typical sibling stuff, but Landon took more verbal abuse than I realized when Hayden started using drugs. Landon was also tired of items disappearing from his room, so he replaced his door handle with one that locked. He was very patient and slow to anger but started to feel some anxiety about what was going on with Hayden and with the changes his friends were making because of the activities they were participating in; Landon was seeing substance abuse all around him. Hayden was encouraging him to try his stuff and now his new friends and some old friends were as well. The pressure got to Landon, and despite what he had been taught and going against his better judgment, he began making poor choices. He started smoking marijuana on occasion and attending parties to drink socially on the weekends to fit in.

Being a smart kid, he was much better at hiding his mishaps. We suspected nothing. He hid it well and continued to do OK at school even though he had been struggling with ADD for years—though we had not taken him in for official evaluation. He told me he was having trouble concentrating at school, but would just deal with it.

At the end of the summer just before his senior year, Landon was hanging out with a few friends who brought beer and marijuana with them to a party. He was given a small amount of marijuana to put in his pocket, and he drank several beers. As the party was ending, a few other people that were there needed a ride home, and Landon gladly said he would drop them off. They all loaded up in Landon's cobalt-blue BMW, and he was on the highway driving to their homes. He was exceeding the speed limit, which caught the attention of a police officer sitting to the side of the road in the dark. As the flashing lights went on and began to move behind Landon, he completely panicked. Instead of just pulling over like he should have, he hit the gas and accelerated.

After about five minutes, his two back tires blew out on a dirt road, and he came to an abrupt stop. He was pulled out of the car and dropped to the ground by the officers, and he yelled, "I messed up." He knew he had made a serious mistake. The officers also pulled out the two ounces of marijuana Landon had in his pocket. Landon didn't realize that at the age of seventeen, he would be charged with a felony for this. He was charged with fleeing from an officer (evading arrest). We got the call from his friend at midnight, letting us know what had happened. We were in shock. Not our other son! Not Landon.

We did not know the extent of his charge until later that next day. He spent the night in a large room with men who were waiting to be placed in jail. Two days later, we picked him up from Collin County jail, and as he climbed into the car, I could feel the tension. He began to explain what had happened and share the details with me. I listened quietly and then began to firmly talk to him about this absurd incident and could not understand why he would ever run from the police. I asked him if he was trying to live out a video game like *Grand Theft Auto* that he used to play. For a moment, I thought maybe I should have never let him play video games! We finished our conversation with him admitting how stupid he had been for his actions. Carl contacted our lawyer to ask for help again because a court date had been set and, unfortunately, we knew how critical going before a judge could be. Landon was put on probation and would be attending monthly visitations with a probation officer and random drug screenings.

Landon's senior year began, and he tried to stay out of trouble and focus on school, but he had difficulties. He and I discussed his attention issue his junior year but never went to a professional for diagnosis. He knew a friend of his was on medication for an attention disorder, so he talked with him about what he used. His friend told him he should try Adderall and gave Landon two of his own pills. Landon swallowed one just before school that morning and left the clear baggie with the other pill in his car in the school parking lot. The drug dogs came to school that day to sniff around, and Landon was pulled out of class after the dogs seemed alert at his car. Possibly due to Hayden's circumstances at this same school, Landon was put on a tighter watch.

Landon called me that morning and said he refused to open the car door for the campus security. I was very surprised by this but began to notice the concern he had in his voice, and I knew there must be something in there. He was already on probation for the incident two months earlier, so I tried to handle the situation as carefully as possible. I arrived quickly at the school parking lot, and Landon was standing there with a police officer and the school's assistant principal. We made the decision not to hand over the keys, in hopes that when the car was towed and removed from the school campus, they could not charge him, but that was not the case. This was when we learned that a controlled substance out of its container and in the hands of someone not prescribed was a felony charge on a school campus. Landon would not release the name of his friend to spare him the consequences of giving out his own medication at school.

At this point, we began to feel numb. Life was starting to seem unreal. Landon was not really processing how damaging all of this was and the lifelong consequences attached to those who receive felonies. Once again, Landon was being charged with a felony at the age of seventeen and had to turn himself in that following morning. When I got in my car, I buried my face in my hands and sobbed. I called Carl to share the bad news and to look to him for strength. Landon would now face a judge with two felonies to his name. It would be a year before his official court date arrived, but he was still on probation. He continued his once-a-month visitation and random drug testing. He was now placed in the Disciplinary Alternative Education Program and had to attend campus in the portable buildings just as Hayden had because he was suspended from school campus.

Carl and I felt ashamed and embarrassed and continued to wonder where we went wrong and why our boys were struggling like this. At this point, we knew Hayden was an addict, but now we were beginning to question Landon. The thought that both our sons would face these challenges the rest of their lives made us sick inside. I began driving Landon to school because we grounded him from his car for several weeks. I dropped him off at the portable buildings for the rest of the semester, and then he was allowed back on campus in the spring to finish his senior year. His grades were up, and he was doing well, even though the thought of his court date was in the back of his mind. All the trouble had set him back, and he decided to stay close and attend the community college to get his basics out of the way instead of applying to a four-year college. He was living at home, so we were able to see him and spend time with him. When someone was on probation, they had very little room for errors, so we continued to remind Landon of this.

Landon began to let his guard down and was socially drinking with college friends. Late one night, he was coming home alone on the dark country road and driving faster than the road allowed. As he approached a large, unmarked curve in the dark, he continued straight ahead and flew into a pasture, busting his back axle and taking down a barbed-wire fence that we were unaware of at the time. Carl got the call from him around midnight and went to help him. When he arrived, he realized Landon had been drinking, and Carl was angry. We just felt lucky we did not have to call the police. The car was towed away, and Landon was brought home. He did not have classes the next morning, so he was still home and sleeping.

About ten the next morning, there was a knock on the front door, so I got up from my desk to look outside. My heart sank as I saw a police car sitting in the driveway. I put a smile on my face and answered the door. The police officer smiled and held up a license plate.

"I think this belongs to you," he said.

In my head, I was thinking, *Oh crap, he left evidence of his wreck.* I explained our son was coming home last night and missed a turn.

In a country voice, he said, "Yes, it happens a lot out there, but did you know he took out a barbed-wire fence? Mr. Jones is tired of it happening. Sometimes his cattle get loose."

I apologized strongly and asked for Mr. Jones's phone number so we could replace it for him. The officer handed me a business card with the phone number on the back, along with the bent license plate. We exchanged good-byes, and I shut the door and turned to breathe. After a few seconds, I could hear the creak of Landon's door as he peeked out from behind it.

"Is he gone? What was that about?" he asked. I held up the bent license plate, and there was no need to say more.

Time passed, and Hayden was not doing well. He was trying to do better and keep up with all of his meetings and his girlfriend but was not using everything he learned to manage his disease of addiction. He was not calling his mentor for support and was not attending the NA meetings like he told us he was. Like all diseases, if you do not do what is prescribed to you, the disease gets stronger and harder to get under control. Hayden did, however, fear going to prison, and he knew if he got caught with anything illegal, they would take him away. We believed that if Hayden was sent to prison, he might not survive. His naive personality and ease with trusting people could get him beat up again.

Since he was feeling the urge to get high, he went back to an old smoke shop he used to go to, where everything was legal and he could buy synthetic drugs, which are substances that are chemically created to mimic the effects of illegal substances like marijuana, cocaine, PCP, and other drugs. Some synthetic substances can be even more harmful than illegal drugs because of how toxic the combination of compounds are; often, they are sprayed with dangerous chemicals and are more potent than their illegal counterparts. But none of those thoughts were present in Hayden's mind. He got a rush thinking about going and what he could find. These shops should not be allowed to be open if they are selling synthetic products, but the way items are labeled and sold, mostly coming from China, the cops cannot just merely shut them down. Hayden arrived there to pick out one of those substances, but with assistance, he was encouraged to try bath salts and bought some packages.

"Bath salts" is the label name for the new designer compound product that contains amphetamine-like chemicals such as MDPV or mephedrone and can be crushed and snorted or swallowed for a high but can quickly deteriorate the brain and body. This product can be ten to fifty times more potent than cocaine and is finally becoming illegal in most states but can still be found on the internet.

Hayden began to use this product daily, mostly at night and in the late evening. He had issues at night that seemed weird at first and became troubling, such as flipping on our bedroom lights around one or two in the morning and standing fully dressed with his laptop in hand, talking out loud that he knew someone had hacked his computer, and he felt he was being watched. He mentioned the FBI must be doing this. Carl took a few minutes to talk with him, calm him down, and get him back to bed. Several nights passed, and this was beginning to be a regular occurrence. Some nights he said he could hear shotgun fire and wondered who was after him. We began to think that after all the drug use, he was now turning psychotic. I checked his room, looking for clues to his behavior, but did not find anything alarming.

After a week of these crazy nightly wake-ups, one morning, I noticed Hayden had a change in color to his skin. I struck up a conversation in the kitchen where the lighting was better and moved close to see him. He looked pale, with a green hue, and his eyes seemed a bit yellow. It was very strange, and I asked him if he felt sick, and he said, "No," in a raspy voice. He did not look or sound all right at all. I called Carl so we could decide what to do. He was at work and suggested I call Hayden's counselor.

Tricia was his counselor at the time because she worked so well with Miranda and knew our family history with Hayden. She came over within the hour, and this was alarming to Hayden. The other kids knew that if Tricia was called over, something was terribly wrong, because she had never paid a visit to the house before. They all stayed upstairs with their doors closed. Hayden did not want to talk to Tricia and denied there were any problems. He proceeded to go in and out of his room. After thirty minutes, I followed him into his room before he was able to shut the door, and it was a disaster. Plates of food and trash covered his desk, along with glasses of milk and juice and soda cans. He had hidden most of his electronics to be "safe from the FBI." His bed was in shambles, with clothes everywhere, and he had hit a few holes in his walls with his fist. I stood in the doorway, trying not to look alarmed. I knew he needed help. I stayed calm and just wanted him to talk to me. He would sit on the bed and doze off for a second and then come back around. I was observing, trying to decide what kind of help he needed. He then jumped up to tell me he had passed out last night in the bathroom and couldn't feel his leg. Tricia felt she could not help him but agreed we should get him to the hospital. I had to be strategic to get Hayden in the car and it took me another hour to convince him. I told the kids I would call later, after I took care of Hayden.

I will never forget the drive to Presbyterian Hospital Plano, which had a mental health and addiction specialty center. This facility was further across town, but we felt he might be going crazy, so I decided to take him there. Carl called and talked with the emergency intake office so they would be aware we were coming. Hayden looked awful, and he grabbed his car keys out of his pocket and scrunched down on the floor of the car. He started yelling that a cop was following us and they wanted to throw him in jail. He put his key up to his throat as if he was going to stab himself and yelled out, "I will fucking kill myself if they do not stop following us."

My heart began to race, and I could feel the anxiety in the car. He pressed the key deeper into his throat as I continued to drive, and I tried to stay calm and convince him differently. I could feel my heart beating rapidly, and I tried not to shake as I gripped the steering wheel. I didn't recognize him as my son. He didn't even look like himself. I held in the tears, but I was terrified. He wanted me to pull over, but I kept driving, knowing I could not take him home. We finally arrived, and I talked to him like he was little kid, in a soft voice.

"Hayden, we are here and everything is okay. Look up, there are no cops anymore. They didn't see you and they are gone."

That ride took everything out of him, and he was weak as he started to get out of the car. I got him admitted, and they put Hayden in ICU. They began running tests and said he was experiencing liver failure and kidney failure, and his body was shutting down. He would have died if we did not get him in there.

Bath salts quickly go to the brain, and they were the reason for his delusions. He slept that first day and had many bags of fluid to get him hydrated and to get his system working again. We had to wait for him to wake up because we had questions for him. What was he using to do this to himself? Because he was on strict probation, we had to be very careful with how we handled this situation and information.

When Hayden felt strong enough to talk, he let us know he was using a new product he purchased, called bath salts. This same substance had been used by another person in Florida, and the guy had hallucinated and chewed a homeless man's cheek off. We remembered hearing about it on the news and were shocked when Hayden said that's what he was using because he could have died.

He said, "I just wanted to see what it felt like," and agreed it was very stupid, and he felt horrible. I remember him asking, "What is wrong with me? Why did I do this?" He knew he needed to go to outpatient therapy and get support. He felt so sick and said he would never do anything like that again.

Hayden's body recovered from the trauma in about two weeks, and his girlfriend was starting to visit again. She knew he had been using the bath salts but was afraid to tell us and jeopardize her relationship with him. She felt ashamed when she found out the substance was quickly killing him. Hayden was without his car now because we took his keys until we thought he could be trusted again. Between the wrecks and this last near-death situation, it would be a while before he could drive again. I became his full-time chauffeur, and that was a daunting task. He also used the commuter train to go down into Dallas to see Natalie. Between him and the other kids, I seemed to be in the car most of the day, driving people around. It was exhausting, and I was trying to stay involved in my hobbies for some relief.

Being in the car with Hayden so much did give us the chance to talk. I will never forget the day he said, "Why me, Mom? Why did I have to get these genetics? I just want to be normal and not have to worry about being an addict all the time. It's hard not to think about using, and people die every day from it. What if I don't make it?" I swallowed hard as he shared his feelings, and I searched for the right words to give him encouragement. I told him to stay strong and follow the tools he had been taught to stay clean. I could tell he doubted himself and lacked confidence. I continued to say everything I could think of that could help and told him to believe in himself. I could tell my words were not having as much impact as I hoped because he changed the subject, and we moved into more lighthearted conversation.

—7—

New Drug

Despite the advice from Enterhealth, Hayden and Natalie were together as much as possible in between keeping up with their daily responsibilities. We were getting to know her and hear about her past. She was a very thin girl with brown hair and brown eyes, and she had a sense of confidence about her. She was friendly, polite to us, and usually wore a smile. Sadly, her mother was a drug user and a bad influence on her. She had legal issues of her own back in Las Vegas, which had gone into warrant status, and she would have to return to deal with them. Hayden was spending time at Natalie's aunt and uncle's home in south Dallas. They had graciously taken Natalie in with hopes of helping her get her life together.

Natalie and Hayden became quite the pair as time went by due to their odd relationship. When they were at our home, we noticed they were starting to argue, and we could hear raised voices behind Hayden's closed door. Later all would seem to be fine and they would laugh and talk again. They were attending NA meetings together and working to stay clean, or so we thought.

Hayden was still feeling the pressures of his felony charges and meetings that were mandatory by the court. He attended an appointment with his probation officer, who informed him it was time for a polygraph test. He would have to take two a year and answer many questions. When Hayden heard "polygraph," he was scared. He was afraid he would fail it for no reason other than nerves. We decided he needed to work with Tricia again and squeeze in a counseling appointment once a week to help him deal with the anxiety and plan the best way to take this kind of test. We also had him back on blood-pressure medication from doctor's orders. I could sense he might be having thoughts of using to escape it all, so I would bring it up to help him talk it out. He would tell me he just wanted a simple life, and he wished he did not have to worry about so much. He just wanted to create music, write lyrics, hold a job, and go back to school, but he felt he had no time to make that happen. Hayden seemed to feel the weight of the world on his shoulders and had trouble believing in himself. Natalie did bring him joy and a sense of acceptance, so he continued their relationship.

The day arrived for Hayden's first polygraph test, and he was a nervous mess. Besides the stress of the test, the office complex he was being sent to was an hour away in a small town. Natalie was going with him in support, so the two of them loaded up, and he could not be late or he would be presumed guilty. Two hours passed and then I heard a car coming up our driveway, so I looked out the front window and, to my surprise, they were already back. They should have been gone about four hours total. Hayden walked in and announced they had gotten lost and could not find the place. I was not happy and knew this could pose great consequences. Luckily, he had called his probation officer during this time, to keep him informed that he had taken a wrong turn and gotten lost. He was offered some grace and told it would be rescheduled for the next week, but if he missed it again, he would go to jail.

I believe this is when the relapse began for he and Natalie both. Neither one of them were strong enough to help the other resist, and the relationship was too close. Everyone knew this was a high-risk relationship, but Hayden and Natalie were too stubborn to believe it. Somehow, somewhere, the drug use began.

It started off slowly and was undetectable but always escalated and gave itself away. They were both beginning to have car wrecks, and the arguing started to increase. We suggested they took time away from each other and put the relationship on hold, but this suggestion was not responded to.

A week passed, and it was time to go back in for the polygraph. This time, I drove Hayden to make sure he made it there. He was not feeling well, and I could see he was sweating and red in the face. During that drive, he confided in me that they would cover the last six months of his life when asking questions, and he had looked at a pop-up porn site that had come across his laptop. He was trying very hard to live up to every expectation and be careful how he was living, which included very limited access to electronics. He was using his laptop to engineer music; therefore, he was using his computer more than he probably should have been. Hayden was always very nervous because his probation officer told him he had no room for error and needed to live carefully. He was embarrassed to tell me about the porn site but said he closed it after a few minutes, and it was adult stuff. He knew they were going to ask many questions about his sexual orientation, so we discussed that he should be up-front so it did not come across as a lie on the test. I left the decision up to him about how he should handle it. He had been following all the rules carefully to uphold the statute of the sex-offense charge except, for this one slipup. I waited in the car while he went inside to be questioned.

About an hour later, he came out and was relieved it was over. The man who gave the test was kind and put Hayden at ease when he got into the room to be hooked up to the lie detector. Hayden talked with him and shared the slipup. He said he appreciated Hayden's honesty and would pass this on to the DA. He told Hayden he passed the test and it would take a month for all the paperwork to clear. The drive home was much more pleasant than the one on the way there. We stopped for lunch and then arrived home.

Days passed and I began to notice a change in Hayden's attitude. I also began to see his regression of organization, a decline in room upkeep, and forgetfulness. He was slowly returning to isolation behind closed doors, even when Natalie was not there. He also had cars I did not recognize stop by the house, and he walked down the road to "talk with them." My heart was sad as I feared his relapse again. I would talk to him about it, and he denied it every time. His probation officer was having him randomly drug tested, so I knew if he was using, it was just a matter of time. I talked to Natalie, but she also denied anything was wrong.

Hayden had another minor car wreck, so we knew it was time to take the keys if he was relapsing. That evening, Carl was furious and felt he should throw Hayden out of the house like other parents had suggested. We told him he needed to leave and figure his life out and hoped a different approach would have an impact on him. The struggle went on for a few minutes, and the other kids just stayed in their rooms. It was upsetting because I knew it was deeply hurting Carl to be physical with Hayden to drag him out of the house. He got him down to the end of the road and ordered him to leave. Hayden began to beg and plead like a child, promising he would get it together and shape up. He followed Carl up the road into the house and into his room. Carl did not want to talk and stayed outside to collect himself and his thoughts.

Later he said to me, "I know we need to have hope, but I'm not sure he's going to make it. He may need more help." I knew I had to start searching his room and his car again.

I was back to driving Hayden to his appointments and meetings because we took his car keys again. He also was forced to take the Dart rail system down into Dallas when he went to see Natalie because I would not drive him down there. One evening, I received a call from Natalie's aunt, and she was very concerned about Hayden. She said he did not seem well and was sitting on the back porch after he and Natalie had a fight. He seemed depressed, and she thought I should come get him. He was not making sense from some of the things he was saying. I decided I better make the hour drive in traffic to pick him up. When I arrived, he did not want to leave their back patio. His behavior was confusing to me, but we finally convinced him to get in the car. He did not want to talk anymore and fell asleep on the way home. I felt sick inside because, from experience, I realized he was using again. I began looking for the clues to understand what was going on.

The next day, I started to search his room and, as I opened the last bottom dresser drawer and lifted some clothes to look under them, I saw a package of needles. As I held up the bag, I sat down on the floor and gasped for air. The only reason he would have these was to inject a drug, and one that was very serious. *No,* I thought. *This cannot be happening.*

Carl was at work, so I decided to wait until he got home to show him what I had found. I talked to Hayden when he arrived home and asked to see his arms, showing him the unused needles I had found. He told me those were Natalie's because she took medication, but I did not believe him. He made up a story and continued to ramble as he went into his room and shut the door without showing me his arms. So that I would not continue to make him angry, I decided to wait until he went to sleep that night to see if I could get a look at his inner arm. Carl and I lay there that night talking about our plan for Hayden and knew we would have to beg the judge to let him leave again for rehab, and this time it would be a long one. The thirty-day to three-month rehabs were not helping at all, and neither were the weekly counseling and NA meetings, which was very upsetting.

After an hour passed, I got out of bed to quietly go into Hayden's room and see if he was sleeping. His days and nights were becoming mixed up again, and sometimes, he stayed up all night and looked terrible the next day. That night, he was actually sleeping, and his bathroom light was on so I could see him in the dark. I slowly pushed open the door and softly walked to the side of his bed. He was lying on his back with his arm stretched up over his head, resting on his pillow. When I leaned down for a better look, the signs were there. I could see needle holes and bruising. I began to tremble and left the room, holding back my tears.

The next morning, Carl called our lawyer and explained the sad news about Hayden's relapse. We finally got Hayden to confess he had been using heroin for several weeks now and knew he could not stop. His desire to use was increasing, and he was needing it more often. I felt sick inside. Carl and I spent several hours looking online, trying to decide where to send him; it had to be for a long time, if the judge would allow it. We found Burning Tree Ranch, a living-facility rehab for the chronic relapser. We studied their site to find very helpful and honest information about relapsing. They encouraged the year-and-a-half program and then believed the next step was a six-month halfway house.

Burning Tree not only focused on addiction but also on behaviors and life skills. They had a starting facility where the very intense and strict policies had to be followed along with meeting all recovery requirements. They were placed on a point system, where very strict and intense policies had to be followed and all recovery requirements met. Once the resident could accomplish everything required, they would graduate to the next, more home-like facility—a large house with living quarters attached—on a ranch. It was expensive, and in addition to the $100,000 already spent for the other rehabs and legal fees, we would probably spend about another $100,000, with high hopes that this time would be a life-changer and beat his disease.

Family involvement and education were strongly recommended for a better chance of success. They were always honest about the low statistics of addicts staying clean. They did feel, because of Hayden's age and severe relapses, he needed some mental testing, but we would have to wait until he was clean and his system was clear. We did not have time to wait and explained the full situation to the director about Hayden's legal situation and the urgency for treatment. She wrote a letter for us to give to the judge and DA, in hopes they would give him the entire stay there that he needed. It took another week for our attorney to get an appointment for Hayden's situation to be heard in front of the judge.

By this time, Hayden was not doing well at all and would have moments of rage and then sadness. His condition was deteriorating fast, and he knew he would have to say good-bye to us and Natalie and be placed in rehab again for a fourth time. He would sit on the edge of his bed and seem like a crazy man, speaking about nothing I could understand. His voice had become raspy, and his eyes looked terrible. He would go in and out of the kitchen, carrying food and drinks to his room that were never consumed. Natalie confessed she was also using heroin, and her aunt and uncle were trying to decide what to do with her. They were both a mess.

We believed the judge could see the desperation in our faces and the illness in Hayden's. Within a matter of a few minutes, and after reading the letters on Hayden's behalf from Burning Tree, Tricia, and his past psychiatrist, he received approval to be sent to Burning Tree Ranch. We were very relieved, but Hayden was still processing his departure. We spent the next day packing and finishing his admittance paperwork. Natalie came over to say good-bye and they made plans to write each other and to stay friends. Earlier, when we had been filling out all of Hayden's admittance papers, we explained his and Natalie's relationship to the counselors at Burning Tree, and they agreed the relationship should have never evolved, and they would not let the communication continue. When Hayden was clean and able to talk with his counselors and have more understanding, they would help him break off the relationship.

The next day, it was time to leave for Burning Tree, but Hayden was angry and telling us he might not go. I kept explaining that the judge signed the form, and he had no choice now. When it was time to load the car and make the drive to Burning Tree, Hayden became difficult. Not only was he leaving us and Natalie behind, but he was also leaving his new drug. He thirsted for another injection, which kept him trapped in emotional turmoil. We spent an hour trying to talk him into the car and reminding him the favor the judge gave him by not sending him to prison. It is always hard to reason with someone who is on drugs. They have a difficult time processing reality, and it is very frustrating. Finally, he got in the car and we were on our way to his new, long awakening.

The first facility was out in a rural area away from town. We were greeted in the parking lot upon entry by two residents who had pro-gressed enough in treatment to receive the privilege of working outside. They took our names and welcomed us. Hayden seemed cold and a little angry to be there. He spent the first week in withdrawal from all of the drug use. Before using heroin, he was using bottles of cough syrups, Natalie's sleeping medication, other stolen prescription drugs, and was even desperate enough to consume a bottle of Valium that had been prescribed to our dog. He had some serious drying out to do before the facility could even reason with him.

They took Hayden to one room for evaluation and Carl and me into another to talk. We discussed all plans and procedures, and then we toured the place. Both of their locations had a full house of residents, and more were expected to come. It was coed, but mostly males were there, ranging in ages from nineteen to fifty. When we heard the age fifty, my heart sank and reminded me that his disease could be lifelong. I could not let that get me down and knew we were doing all we could to help him, but it was up to him to help himself. We hugged Hayden goodbye and said some positive words of encouragement, even though he was not absorbing our conversation. He stood in the doorway and watched us leave, knowing it would be about a month before we saw him again. He would have time to come clean and clear his head first. We would actually be able to talk to him and see more of his real personality again. As I turned to look back, my emotions overcame me, but I also felt relief knowing home would be more peaceful now.

As Carl and I drove home, I sat quietly thinking about Hayden and all of our shattered expectations. I thought about the destruction of his body and brain from all the substance abuse and wondered if he could heal and come back to us. My heart longed for his purity as a child again. His disease was robbing him of peace and happiness. My dreams played again in my head, and I wondered if this was God's way of warning us of what was to come. I began to see Hayden's disease as the devil, wrapping around his body like the grotesque figure in my dream to make him weak and relapse. *Is this the battle between good and evil?* I wondered.

The Bible says the devil preys on the spiritually strong and tries to break them and consume everything they love, so maybe the devil was trying to break me by taking our son away from us. I wanted answers but knew all I could do was stay strong and keep having faith in God because he knew Hayden's struggles and still loved him.

Dealing with addicted loved ones can tear families apart. Many rehab parent meetings Carl and I attended were often filled with sad, separated couples who blamed each other for the destruction in their family. We witnessed many arguments and tears from pain and heartbreak. Addiction is hard to understand and extremely frustrating because life will never be the way you imagined it would be. It is up to the addict to stay on track with treatment and to be open and honest about what they feel inside. It did become apparent to us that the addicts with more stubborn traits and personalities had a harder time staying clean. They were too stubborn to believe how sick they were and therefore often resistant to treatment. It only took one unmanaged thought to send an addict spiraling into relapse. Day after day, a fine line was walked; then, added stress could trigger a thirst also called craving. You may have heard the phrase, "One day at a time" from the twelve-step recovery program. This can be effective as long as the addict believes in the treatment and has come to the conclusion that they need it. We had some great family times when Hayden was clean and following his plan. It became normal, however, to live on an emotional roller coaster.

—8—

Prison

The house was calm, and we were starting to catch our breath after getting Hayden settled into his new living arrangements at Burning Tree Ranch. I began the task of cleaning out Hayden's room and bathroom, which had turned into a dump yard during the last few weeks he was home. He had even punched a few holes in the wall. Food and drinks had been spilt and trash not picked up. The furniture was worn and the drapes torn. It made me very sad to see the destruction but relieved that it was over.

I completely stripped down the room and had the bedroom suite picked up and hauled away. I was having the room repaired, repainted, and refurnished to turn it into a guest bedroom. We agreed that Hayden could not be allowed to move back home.

The girls were looking forward to summer and excited about our family vacation to Costa Rica. Miranda had been hard at work during this semester at school, and she was finishing her junior year ahead of schedule. She was doing very well and decided to go back to Lovejoy High School her senior year and try out for cheerleading. She was a cheerleader in ninth grade before she left and had enjoyed that part of school, so she decided to sign up for gymnastics again to brush up on her tumbling skills to be ready for tryouts. Miranda missed her relationship with Hayden and wished he did not have to leave for help again, but she knew he really needed it. Olivia was fully aware of most everything we had been struggling with, and I knew, at her age, that was a lot to process. We would talk about Hayden's disease, and she knew about Miranda's cutting, but the sex-offense charge would stay a secret. She was too young to be told the details. Olivia was a smart girl and always brought us joy. She was doing well playing volleyball, and I was glad she found a new passion.

Landon was finishing up a semester at a community college that was close to us. He was still attending his monthly probation meetings and required drug testing because of his felony charges. He took care of his responsibilities with much more ease than Hayden ever did. College, however, was not enjoyable for him, and he was not living up to his potential. He was discouraged, having to sit through long English and history classes. His attention was not there, and he was trying to figure out what he wanted to do about school. Because of his felony charges, he was only allowed a certain distance away from the county, and he felt limited. He kept in contact with a few friends whom he should not have had in high school, but they still lived in the area. These friends had been at parties, had smoked pot in the past, and had been involved in a fight with other kids.

One evening, Landon was home upstairs doing what he loved, which was working on an electrical project. He received a call from one of his old friends named Kenny, who was actually a nice kid from a good family, who got caught up in smoking and selling marijuana in high school. Landon had not heard from Kenny in six months because his parents were being stricter on him, and we believed he was doing well. Landon was surprised to get the call from him, and they talked briefly. He invited Landon to go to dinner. Landon, missing his friend, gladly took him up on the offer. Kenny offered to pick him up, and Landon said sure.

Landon told me his plans and said he would be back in two hours. I was glad they could catch up and believed Kenny was doing well. Kenny arrived, Landon yelled, "Bye, Mom!" and the front door shut.

As they drove away, casual conversation started, and they were exchanging information about the past six months to catch up, Landon told me. Halfway to their dinner destination, Kenny quickly announced that he needed to make a delivery, and it would just take a second. To Landon's surprise, as Kenny was turning into a neighborhood, he pulled a large plastic sack of marijuana from under the seat. Landon sat there, not saying much, as Kenny pulled over to a curb to get out of the car.

Within a minute, lights began flashing and a police officer pulled up behind Kenny's car, and Landon sat there in disbelief. He had no room for error, and even though he had nothing to do with the bag of marijuana Kenny was selling, he could be arrested for being there because of his felony charges. He held up his hands and let them know he just got picked up and was not a part of this deal. All we could assume was Kenny was under suspicion for past situations and the police were on the lookout for his car. Kenny was arrested, and he and Landon were taken to jail. Landon would possibly face a misdemeanor charge for being in the car and near the deal, which broke probation rules. When I got the call from Landon, I could hear great frustration in his voice. He could not believe what had just happened. Kenny knew Landon had his own charges but did not think twice about getting caught and putting Landon in this serious situation.

I was furious and headed out for the police station to beg on Landon's behalf. I explained what I knew and begged for his release. They would not grant it to me but smiled and said he would be checked in to Collin County, and we could pay bond and pick him up there. I left angrily but had to keep my composure. I knew this was just plain bad luck for Landon.

When I picked him up the next day, he was upset. We arrived home and sat out on the front porch to talk. He was full of emotion and said he needed to go away somewhere. I turned to look at my 6'2" boy. He had tears in his eyes and added, "I can't keep dealing with all this."

Landon tended to hold everything inside and did not talk much about his feelings. He never talked of Hayden, but I knew it was hard on him to feel like he had lost his brother. They had barely had contact in the past six months, and one of those times, he was sticking up for me when Hayden was a bit out of control. To hear Landon say, "I want to go away and get help" was serious. I felt his bottled-up emotions were about to blow.

We received word from our lawyer that a new court date was set for Landon. It was a few months away, which gave us time to figure out a plan for him. We found a Christian group that helped young adults in distress. They provided counseling, group meetings, and outdoor excursions to teach endurance and coping skills during a two-month program. Then, we wanted to send him to a supervised life-coaching school in California that was accredited and focused on life-skills management and communication, well-being, and healthy living, along with substance counseling if they felt it was necessary after psychological and reasoning testing. It was a yearlong, structured program, and then he could go to full-time college in the area. It was a great fit for him because he could continue school. We would just need approval from the judge, and his charges would need to be transferred to the state of California, and he would need to be monitored there by a new probation officer. The school wrote letters explaining the experience they had with situations like Landon's and the connection they had with the court system to ensure he would follow court orders. Our lawyer felt very confident in this plan for Landon, so we prepared for the transition.

We took our family vacation to Costa Rica, and Landon came with us. We had an amazing time there. It was very relaxing to get away and enjoy the ocean and the beautiful sky at night. We all spent hours talking and laughing and going on excursions together. Landon loved the beach, so he spent a great deal of time in the water, wrestling the waves that crashed in. He came out like a drowned rat, with a smile on his face, wiping away the sand and water. After seven days, we caught a flight home and back to reality.

Our lawyer advised us to start Landon's two-month program in the mountains. Even though we did not have approval yet, he felt the judge would leave Landon in a program he had already started. He believed the judge would approve a structured plan and grant Landon the help because he had just turned nineteen. We had letters and documents that proved Landon could make a smooth transition. Landon had agreed to all of this and was looking forward to a new start in a new place. We packed everything he needed and flew him to the mountains of North Carolina, where a great group of people met and greeted him. The downside was he would have to return to Texas in three weeks. The program rarely allowed this due to the timing and planning of their program, but they understood his situation and wanted to help as much as possible. During his first two weeks, I received a call from a counselor who had spent time talking with Landon and helped him open up. She said he was such a polite kid and asked if he was normally a cryer. She told me that Landon shared a lot and also cried a lot as well. I was very relieved because I knew it was just what he needed to do, and he felt safe there to talk about life and everything we had been through.

She said, "I can tell when these guys are being real or not, and Landon definitely is."

He had a workbook that he wrote in as well as books to read. He was able to go out on one mountain excursion before we had to fly him home for his court date in Texas. We were planning to have him back up to North Carolina by the next day to resume his schedule. Landon arrived in good spirits and gave me a big hug. It was good to see him. We had him put on his dress clothes to look nice for court. I was a little nervous but felt we had a great plan in place for him. Carl and I were both there that day, in support.

There were a few court hearings before Landon's, so we waited for about two hours and then were allowed in, as the case before ours was about to finish. A few law students sat in chairs along the wall near the middle of the court room for observation and education purposes. We could tell the case before ours was offering some challenges to the judge, and it was running long.

Landon's time arrived to go up to the bench in front of the judge with his lawyer, and I could feel a churning in my stomach and my heart rate increase. Carl and I sat there very quietly, holding hands. Our lawyer began talking and discussing Landon's charges and the plan we could offer in support of Landon and his need for mental support. The judge looked at Landon and read out his past charges. He then asked Landon several questions and made it very clear he was not happy with his past behavior. Our lawyer presented the letters from the school in California and explained the program Landon was committed to for help, mental growth, and continuing education and also shared the current program he was attending. The judge sat quietly with his head down, thinking.

This judge was also familiar with Hayden's case, which was not helpful to Landon. We were in the same courthouse we always went to for Hayden's issues, and he was given many chances.

We all sat there, waiting for the verdict, and I remember feeling a little dizzy. After a few minutes, the judge looked up at Landon and said he believed Landon needed to serve some time and ordered him to six months in state prison. I turned to Carl and asked what the judge said because I did not think I heard him right. Carl gripped my hand and arm and whispered, "He is sending him to prison." I looked up as the guards came to Landon's side with handcuffs. I yelled out, "No, please wait! Let me take the stand please and talk." I started sobbing heavily. Landon turned back to look at me, and all we could do was have a last-minute stare into each other's eyes before he was handcuffed and taken away.

I did not even get to hug him, so I yelled again, and the judge looked up with a gentle smile and shook his head no. He said, "The court rests," and slammed down the mallet.

At this point, Carl was trying to calm me down as we sat there, almost paralyzed by what had just happened. Our lawyer was stunned, and Tricia was there in support, and neither of them knew what to say. They were speechless for a moment.

As I tried to stand, my legs were weak, and I could not stop crying. Carl lifted me out of my chair to help me to the small room we were meeting in with our lawyer and Tricia behind the courtroom. As we walked in, they closed the door behind us and started apologizing and trying to bring sense to what had happened. Our lawyer could hear and see what a mess we were in and began to try to lighten the situation. He explained it would go fast for Landon and because of his age, he would probably be transferred to a state jail that didn't house hard criminals. He said the clock started ticking right away, and he would probably spend the first month in Collin County jail while they processed all his paperwork, as the government works slowly. His next thought was that Landon would be placed in a location close to the Dallas metroplex that would make it easy for visitation. He continued to talk, but I lost focus and could no longer hear his words. I just kept picturing Landon's lifeless face as we made our last eye contact. My heart felt as if it had been slashed in half. More pain and confusion, more suffering and heartache. The unthinkable was now a thought that we did not want. At age nineteen, our son would serve prison time.

The last incident, when he was in the wrong place at the wrong time, with Kenny, must have put the judge over the edge. Carl managed to keep himself together and be strong for me. He helped me out of the courthouse, and we drove home.

Phone calls had to be made to both programs to share our bad news that Landon was denied release to them and would be locked up instead. They were very sorry to hear the news and knew there was nothing they could do. As I tried to explain everything to the girls, I once again cried, and they hugged me tight. Hours passed before I received that first phone call from Landon. I answered my phone and accepted the collect call. As I said hello, a voice said "Mom?"

Holding back the tears I said, "Landon, where are you, honey?"

I could tell he started to cry a bit, and he said, "I'm in jail, Mom."

We cried for a moment together, and I searched for the right words to say. "I am sorry, Landon; I never imagined it would happen this way. You are going to be okay. I know you are strong, and we are here for you."

He was still waiting to have his paperwork transferred from the court, so he was put in a large room with other detainees for twenty-four hours. He did not sleep during that time but was fed and given water. Our time was up and he had to get off the phone so someone else could make a call. We said our good-byes, and I knew he had to wipe his face and pull his emotions together before he turned around to face the room. I just wanted the next day to arrive so he could call us back. Carl wanted to talk with him to say some positive words of encouragement.

That evening, I took the girls to the nail salon because I needed to get my mind off what happened that morning in court. I kept playing the court scene over and over in my head, and I would see that mallet slam down. The girls were trying to be supportive but knew I was making a strong effort not to think. Carl went into work that afternoon to consume himself with phone calls and meetings. When he arrived home, we hugged and began to talk and look online to find out information on Texas state jails and prisons. That is one area we knew very little about other than what we had seen on television, in the news, or in the movies. Since our lawyer felt he would be close, we focused on the ones within an hour away, hoping it would be Hutchins State Jail, which was an hour away. We began to read about the system and the process, as well as living conditions and what he would able to do while he was in there. Visitation would be limited, and so would phone calls, which meant I would be writing a lot of letters. We also realized he would spend Thanksgiving and Christmas in there, but he would be finishing up six months and possibly be home for the New Year or just after. This would be the first year both boys would not be home for the holidays. I did not want to think about it, so I pushed on to other thoughts.

The next day, Landon's call came through, and we were relieved to hear from him. He spoke softly, and I could tell he was lacking energy.

He explained what all was happening, which was not much yet. He was exhausted and ready to sleep. I passed the phone to Carl so he could talk to him and hear his voice. We shared our thoughts with him and where we assumed he might be transferred to. We encouraged him to get involved in whatever he could and volunteer to make time pass fast. He agreed and said he would know as soon as they gave him the list after he was placed in a cell. This was the same jail that Hayden was punched in the face and had his jaw broken in. It did make me nervous, but because Landon had a much different personality than Hayden, I felt he could handle himself better. He was more of a thinker than a socializer. I knew he would keep a low profile in there, and he had a confidence about himself that Hayden never had. I still knew the risks in state prison had to be greater than in county jail. Landon told us they informed him that he would not know when he was being transferred for security purposes. We had no idea when he would be leaving, and we would have to wait for a phone call. Three weeks into the process, a week went by and we knew he must have been moved. We set up a call-in account for him, and he was not using it, so we had to wait and wonder where he was.

After a week passed, we finally heard from him. To our surprise, he was three hours away from us, in the Gurney Correctional Institute unit in Palestine, Texas. He made a stop and spent a few nights in the Huntsville Unit and then was transferred out again. He explained to me how the prisoners left Collin County jail in the middle of the night, all chained together and loaded on a van. He said they did this to make it harder for anyone to receive help in escaping.

All transfers were kept secret for security purposes. He had no idea where he was going and the ride was dark and long. As they approached Huntsville, the sun was starting to rise to light up the day. Landon looked out the window to see his first stop and was surprised to see a very high fence, topped with massive hot wire, wrapped around the entire complex. By the look, he could tell this was maximum security where very serious criminals were placed. Some were there with life sentences.

Landon, with the other convicts, were herded inside like cattle. Each detainee was strip-searched and given one minute and a bar of soap to shower in freezing cold water to clean off before sent to the holding cell to await placement. He was not allowed to make any phone calls. Some stayed at this facility, and others, like Landon, were moved on. By day two, Landon was awakened again during the night and made the drive to Gurney Transfer Facility, which is also a maximum-security facility. He was strip-searched again, told to clean up, and forced to wait, unclothed, for two hours in a holding room. Once he was placed in a cell, he knew this was where he would stay to live out his sentence. The strip searches went on three times a week for the first month he was there. He was glad he was allowed to leave his boxers on and the process shortened as time passed. He was processed in and assigned a cell along with another inmate and spent the next six months there.

—9—

Visitation

It was a busy six months with the girls back in school and with Miranda in her senior year. She made cheerleader, and, in between school and sports, she had a full schedule. She was driving now, which was a huge help.

Olivia had her usual activities and loads of friends. The house was calm, and now Landon's room was empty and I kept it in order like he left it. Carl and I were still leaning on each other for support and resumed date nights to keep our relationship strong. We made time to enjoy each other and talk about the positives in our lives. This was very important to keep our relationship strong and healthy.

On occasion to lighten things up, one of us would make the joke that if the other one left they had to take the kids. We would both laugh and say, well I'm not leaving! We would look at each other, shaking our heads, and discuss why this was happening to our family. We loved our sons and prayed they would find peace. We began planning our schedules and coordinating weekends to be sure not to miss visitation opportunities for both boys. Hayden accomplished all of the steps at the first Burning Tree location, which was not easy for him. He had to be organized and responsible, as well as open and honest, to get through the first months of private and group meetings. He had a checklist to accomplish and he was proud of himself to have completed it within six months.

He moved to Kaufman, where the larger Burning Tree Ranch home was located. It was a nicer place to live and grow, with much supervision and guidance. The staff was amazing, professional, warm, and caring. Helping others find a healthier mental state and many tools to use to stay clean was their ultimate goal. They also focused on life skills and teaching the residents how to live, cook, and clean. Despite all their planning, teaching, organizing, and counseling with great effort, they would be honest with families and tell us the statistics were low for addicts to stay clean forever, but with long-term care the stats increased for their residents.

They educated families as well, and we attended every visitation and family weekend. Studies showed that if the families were more educated about the disease, it increased the chances for their loved one to be successful.

They built a community there on the ranch and everyone had jobs that would rotate weekly for learning purposes. Hayden would experience another structured year at this location, and we knew from experience that Burning Tree was different and honest. The other rehabs were too short and costly for the time he spent there. We wished we'd found Burning Tree years earlier when Hayden had had less relapses to his name and could have avoided his felony situation, but we could only look forward.

Burning Tree made sure we knew not to blame ourselves for Hayden's condition and assured us genetics played a huge part in his disease. The difficulty lay in trying not to be enablers, which many of us living with an addicted loved one had been guilty of at one time or another. The enabling behavior was what drove most parents apart because many times, one parent would give in to the deception of the addict and take a blind eye to what was really going on or did not want to believe the problem existed. When Carl and I first became aware of the title "enabler," it caught our attention because it reminded us of some of the situations we had been in. We had had no idea in the first couple of years what we were doing and no idea what Hayden was doing; until they are educated about addiction, most people have no idea how to deal with addicts. I began to realize how important early education and real understanding was for students and parents on the subject of addiction. This subject wasn't discussed enough, and many people were in the dark. A day did not pass that I did not think about Hayden because he was always on my mind, and I was so glad he was safe at Burning Tree.

And then, I had another vivid dream about Hayden while he was there.

THIRD DREAM: COLLISION

I was suspended in air like an out-of-body experience watching the black and white scene below. It was a cold dark night and I saw Hayden behind the wheel of a car, driving down a very dark road. I turned in slow motion to look in the direction he was driving, to see what was up ahead for him. My heart began to race as I saw a huge ghostly demon draped in torn rags with arms open and mouth fully extended wide, flying ferociously, full speed, toward Hayden. It was much larger than him and his car. The bottom jaw of the horrible figure dropped open with fangs dripping, and as it collided with Hayden like an explosion, I jumped, my eyes opened, and I lay still, thinking about what I just dreamed.

It felt so real, like the other two dreams, and I knew I would never forget it. I just wanted to understand it. I was going to wake Carl but decided to tell him the next morning. As I shared the dream with him, he asked what I thought it meant. I thought for a bit, and I said, "Oh my goodness; this has to mean he defeated his demon and killed it."

We would, at times, call addiction a demon because of its possessive nature. *He can stay clean,* I thought. Carl smiled and agreed it was possible. I shared the dream with the girls and looked forward to telling Hayden.

Before Landon was sent away, we all had a chance to attend the family weekend visitation. It was a cookout and also included games, a speaker, a funny skit, and family talk time. Hayden had been clean for seven months, and he was clear-headed and seemed his self again. We enjoyed every minute of the day because every day with someone in recovery becomes special. He was so glad we were all there.

He also apologized for not being a better big brother. He was beginning to understand all we were going through and beginning to understand himself better. It still bothered him that he was the one with this disease and not "normal." He gave encouraging words to Landon about his charges and told him to be good and stay away from drugs. He spent time with Miranda and Olivia listening to what was going on in their lives. At this point, he knew we were going on family vacation to Costa Rica and hated to miss out.

We all ate dinner and then watched the funny skit he was in about rehabs and Hollywood stars. He was playing the rapper Eminem in the skit and wrote a rap which he performed. It was funny and amusing and had everyone laughing. As night set in, we listened to a speaker and enjoyed a bonfire. Before we said our goodbyes, exchanged hugs, and returned home, I sat down with Hayden to share my dream. He found it very entertaining and interesting. I told him what I thought it meant, and he was glad to hear the news that he defeated his demon.

A few weeks passed, and Carl and I returned for the required family therapy weekend. They encouraged only parents, spouses, and older siblings to attend this intense weekend. We spent two days in group settings and group meetings with Hayden and other residents with their families. Everything and anything applying to an addict and their disease could be discussed. So much hurt and confusion filled the room. One particular session required everyone to write down their feelings about the guilt they felt and what they wished they had done differently. As I sat knee-to-knee with Hayden, looked into his eyes, and shared my list, he reassured me to have no guilt. He told me he loved me and not to blame myself for anything. It was a hard session to get through, and Carl had to do the same. We learned so much that weekend and were able to find healing. Hayden also confided in us about different life-threatening situations he'd been in to get drugs.

Now that he had been clean for this long, looking back, he could not believe what his disease had driven him to do. He shared a story about needing a fix and had been told of a secret crack house he could go to. The house was in a back street of Oak Cliff, just south of Dallas. It was in a rough neighborhood, but this had never stopped Hayden before. As he walked in to make a purchase, a cocked gun was put to his head. They did not recognize him, and he was also a white boy. The dealer began asking him questions in a raised voice, and Hayden knew he better have quick answers. He managed to say what they needed to hear, about how he had been sent there and that he could pay for what they were dealing. Hayden was shaken up but kept his cool and got what he needed. He said, "Mom, I could have been shot that day."

After sitting there listening to that story and a few others of his, I began to understand the sickness and desperation he felt.

The analogy that drugs to an addict is like water to someone dehydrated and dying of thirst made sense. Addicts feel like they cannot survive without using, which was why it was so difficult to control their thoughts. I remember wondering for the first time if brain surgery was on option for treatment and decided to do my own research on that when we returned home. We finished up group meetings that afternoon and stayed for dinner. Carl and I took time to visit with the other parents and engaged in casual conversation, which usually ended up in deep conversation about what tragedies had occurred in our lives. Carl and I were so glad we had been a team on this long, hard journey together because so many were alone and facing it without their partner. Some were there together but full of anger. The cost and how much money we had all spent to get our loved one clean also came up. Most of us had already spent over $100,000, and I thought about so many who probably needed help but their families could not afford it. We felt blessed that we were able to help Hayden.

At dinner, as we sat around the big room with long tables, Hayden would yell out something funny to one of his new friends and introduce us. They were all friendly and ready to share their goals in life and hobbies they enjoyed. All of them wanted a better life and to be able to stay clean. They were making plans and looking forward to success.

Hayden's favorite friend was Pete, a big, burly kid, who was an artist and had a great sense of humor. He and Hayden became friends quickly. They were close in age, with Pete just one year older. They had similar personalities and both had a stubborn streak. There were always a few who were more concerning than others and Hayden and Pete made it onto that list. The counselor let us know they could tell by personality who might take longer in treatment and took more planning for after release, but we would discuss that as Hayden progressed through the program.

We finished dinner and said our good-byes. We would return the next day for day two, to finish family therapy and hug Hayden before our departure. We told Hayden about Landon's sentence to prison, and he was sick inside. He actually could not believe it and felt some responsibility because of everything that'd happened. He wished he had been a better brother and that things had been different. We assured him Landon loved him and never once blamed him for anything. We finished hugging and assured him we would return for the next visitation in three weeks.

—10—

Frustration

Landon's visitation at Gurney Transfer Facility was quite different from Hayden's family visitation. The inmates were given visitation through a number system and Landon's had finally arrived. It had been two months since we'd seen or spoken with him. The only way we knew where he had been placed was through a letter he was able to send. We were surprised to hear the name Gurney because it did not match any of the expected locations. As we researched and found out it was three hours away and held as many as two-thousand inmates on a range of charges from Landon's to hard criminals facing life sentences, we called our lawyer, who apologized but said Landon would be okay and that it could have been worse. That answer, of course, hadn't made us feel any better. I wrote Landon back immediately to let him know we would see him soon and to be careful.

We had an online list of steps to be taken to ensure we would be able to see Landon. We knew it made sense because this was a maximum-security facility. I was actually glad at that point to see tight restrictions in place, knowing it was better for Landon and his safety while in there. Carl and I gathered all the documents we needed, cleaned out the car free of any extra items, dressed properly, looked for the best way to get there, and headed down the road early in the morning. We read that the process just to get in to the prison was a long one and we should get there early to get in line. We left at 5:30 am for the three-hour drive. We talked all the way there, which made time pass quickly and helped my nerves to calm down. As we approached the area, we finally found the first checkpoint, which was not well-marked. A few cars were in line, and they spaced us out to do a full car inspection in, around, and under the car to make sure nothing was coming in with us that should not be there. Once that was completed, we were given a number and some information and were showed the dirt lot we were to wait in. *Well that wasn't too bad*, we thought, it only took twenty minutes to check in. So, we sat on a lot, looking around at all the other cars there with approved guests sitting inside them. There was a range of cultures and classes of people. On occasion, we watched some people pull off the lot and drive up the road to where the facility was. We could not see it from where we were sitting. After forty-five minutes, our number was finally called and we were looking forward to seeing Landon.

We drove to the parking lot and saw the facility for the first time. It was very large and gray, with very tall fences that had electric wires balled up all the way around it. Yes, it was a very serious place—and one I thought we would never see firsthand. We got out of the car to find our number only gave us a place in the next line, which had about fifteen people waiting in it. We took our place and struck up little conversation with those around us.

One woman stood out who was tall attractive and blond. She had a sadness about her as she spoke that she had been there many times to see her husband. They had seen some hard-financial times, and he was stealing money to help them live. They had a child that she was fully responsible for now. He was serving a ten-year sentence and had been there for three of it. The strain of his decisions was apparent on her face, but she loved him and just wanted him back home with the family.

Others were there with children who were coming to visit their dad and the way they laughed and played made it clear this was a normal part of life for them. Even though Carl and I felt very out of place, we put away our pride and realized no one there was going to judge us. We were just another family who had come to support the one they loved.

The wait in line became long, and we felt we might not get in before visitation closed. That scenario was possible because rules were strict and they didn't care how long you had been waiting in line. They could cut it off whenever they felt enough were passed in. I would have been angry if we were turned away, so I was glad we were almost to the check-in office.

Inside the small office sat two women who were checking IDs and all documents so that we could be approved for visitation. They could pass or deny our access. Once we passed their station, we were sent into the frisking room for our pat-down, told to use the bathroom there if we needed to go, and given another number for entry. We exited into a small, wired courtyard with large security cameras and waited in line again. Three hours had passed since we first drove up, but it was finally time to go in to visit with Landon. As we walked through the door, we entered into another line to get into the plain white room that had the appearance of a small cafeteria with only vending machines. We got approval at the desk and were assigned to a table.

During all of the time we were trying to get in, Landon had been notified we were on-site, and he was placed in another area for those who had visitors. Sadly, many did not have visitors because their families had given up on them. We waited another ten minutes and we could see Landon making his way in. His head was shaved, and he was wearing a blue jumpsuit with white Velcro tennis shoes. The shoes could have no strings to keep inmates from hanging themselves or strangling someone else. That was an awful thought, even though it made sense.

We stood up to hug him, and it felt good to be holding my big boy again. He seemed a bit uncomfortable that we had to be there, but we quickly struck up conversation to utilize the hour we had with him. He had already seen and heard a lot in there and was quickly learning how to handle himself. To his advantage, he was tall and stout, which made him seem tougher than he was. Don't get me wrong, he was strong, and with a year of mixed martial arts under his belt, he could very well defend himself if needed, but he had a kind heart, which was a character kept secret in there. He was in the smallest ethnic ratio. Not many white boys, which also made him stand out. His cellmate was not too bad, just talked a lot so Landon politely listened.

The two months seemed slow, and Landon was very glad he only had four more to go. He shared that he had jobs, which allowed him time out of his cell. His least favorite was being in the chain gang that was taken outdoors and given tools to work the soil for farming. He preferred doing laundry or dishes. He attended the church service that came once a week, with music and a speaker. A workbook was also given to him that had to be completed along with an eleven-week class before he could start approval to exit Gurney.

The hardest part was the crazy sleep and awake hours that constantly changed due to the large number of inmates. Sometimes he would be awakened to eat breakfast at three in the morning. All the lights would be flipped on and a small amount of time was given to get in line if you wanted to eat. The bathroom set up was also a terrible experience. It was all open area, with showers and toilets next to each other. Landon felt as if he took his poop in the middle of the room. It got easier as time went by, but was still awful.

We shared what all was going on with us and the rest of the family and talked of how we were so glad he had come on that last trip to Costa Rica. We encouraged him to focus on the positives in his life and the good memories. We discussed what reading material he wanted so I could send him books. I could not mail any books directly, but I could order them and have them mailed from an approved trusted source on Gurney's list.

It was hard to say good-bye when our hour was up. We cleaned the table from the trash and soda cans we'd bought from the vending machine. The vending machines offered items he could not get in prison, so he was glad for the treats. We hugged him and watched him exit the room and disappear into a dim hallway. Like cattle, we were herded out to completely exit the compound. Every move we made was highly supervised. We got to our car, which was inspected again on departure, and slowly drove away to make the three-hour drive home.

I thought about Landon and how he needed intellectual stimulation, so I spent hours looking for books with educational information, as well as beautiful pictures and interesting facts, to send to him. I also began writing letters daily and sending positive messages and song lyrics for him to read. He was going to be in Gurney during Christmas, and we also received word his projected release date was in late January. We were disappointed to hear the news but knew there was nothing we could do.

As the holidays drew near, I began to shop and plan for the kids. We would take Hayden's present to him at the holiday visitation, and I would mail Landon's books to him. The girls' gifts would be placed under the tree and we would take them with us to visit family around Christmas. It was so strange to think about the kind of holidays the boys had grown up with and where they were spending them this year. It did not seem real and cast a sadness on the holidays.

Landon called after receiving his books, which had arrived early, about a week before Christmas. He was thankful, but we laughed as he said, "Hey Mom, thanks for my books." He had never received books for Christmas nor had he ever asked for any. Books were an item he'd bought whenever he needed them, but now they had become a luxury to take his mind off the cold cell he spent many hours a day in.

Hayden was able to unwrap his gifts with us there at Burning Tree. He loved jewelry, so we bought him a watch along with some other smaller gifts. He was appreciative and glad we came down again for another visit.

The holidays passed, and a new year arrived. Hayden was progressing well, and they were planning his next phase to move into a halfway house. They decided it was best to separate him from the others he had developed a close friendship with. His friends were to be released before him to the usual halfway house, but Hayden would go to a more structured one about thirty minutes away from his friends. The clinical director's intuition and experience led her to these decisions, and we supported them. The ultimate goal was to give all graduated residents the best chance with the right living arrangements. So, Pete and Hayden's other friends graduated and moved into the halfway house in north Dallas. Hayden felt good and was looking forward to graduating but was moving slow to finish his last section of work. He also was looking for a mentor because this was required upon exit. Mentors were people who understood everything the addict thought and felt because they themselves were recovering addicts who had been clean for at least three years. Hayden would call his mentor for guidance and support after he moved into the halfway house.

The end of January arrived, and we helped Hayden move into his new home at the halfway house and were waiting to hear from Landon about his release date from prison. It had been seven months since he had been incarcerated, and we were ready to bring him home. He was having trouble sleeping and began feeling anxious to leave. He had witnessed many situations from the Gurney inmates—everything from fistfights to penis implants, which seemed crazy. He could not believe the pain and risk the guys would take to get prohibited tattoos and penis implants before they were released. If caught, they would have many years added to their sentence. They felt it was worth the risk to make their ladies respect them.

Landon managed to mind his own business but had figured out the art of trade if someone wanted something from him. Extra food and toiletries were a luxury, and many inmates did not have a cash account set up, which they could spend at the vendor window to get what they wanted. We established an account for Landon, knowing he would need extra food and items. One trade he made was for my birthday. He met a guy who was an artist and asked him to draw a picture of me with balloons on the outside of my birthday card and a picture of Landon on the inside. A few days before my birthday, I received it, and it brought me to tears. Not only had he remembered my birthday, but he had put creative thought into it as well. He was able to give the artist a picture of me that I had mailed him to do the drawing from. I was so delighted but could not personally thank him until he called me a few days later. It was February now, and he was still waiting to be released. We called our lawyer, but there was nothing he could do, and he reminded us that the government moves slowly with paperwork. Landon continued to stay as busy as he could, but it was hard. He had completed his workbook and the required class weeks before. I continued to write and send pictures to help keep his spirits up. Carl and I took turns talking to him when he could call.

Hayden was managing his probation meetings and was required to start the sex-offender meetings again. He was clear-headed and had gained some maturity during the past year but was dreading those meetings. He was attending NA meetings and had found a mentor. He also had supervision while he lived at the halfway house. He found a part-time job and had applied to a small private college to attend and began working on his audio-engineering degree. After he was approved because of his charges, he was able to start attending a class. He decided to take it slow because he had been out of school for so long. He had requirements that had to be accomplished as house rules, but Hayden was struggling with organization and trying to manage his meetings, work, and school. They continued to make sure he took his recovery seriously but were concerned he was putting everything else before that. He continued to push forward and slowly get better at management. He was feeling better about himself and gaining some confidence. He was attending huge AA/NA meetings and even spoke one evening, trying to help those new to being clean. He was so proud to be clean for a year and a half. Carl and I were glad everything seemed to be going better for him. We did know he would have to work hard for the rest of his life to stay sober.

His probation officer had been looking through his file and came across the polygraph test Hayden took before he left to go to Burning Tree and was reminded about the notes left by the district attorney. She wanted to be sure Hayden served his three weeks in jail for the little slipup he confessed to the examiner. This punishment was yet to come and surprised us all.

—11—

Coming Home

We lost contact with Landon and assumed he must be on the move back to Dallas for us to pick him up somewhere. He had not been given any indication of when he would be leaving but told us his release date was coming soon. His six-month sentence had turned into eight at this point. We knew if we did not hear from him in three or four days he was not able to call. We were looking forward to his return and for his life to start again. He was making plans to get back in school and focus on engineering. Because he served time in prison, his probation was over. He would, however, have a felony attached to his name. Life would be more difficult when looking for a place to live, when getting accepted to school, or when getting hired. We knew Landon was smart and had a confidence about him that would help him find success. He would return to us a different person because of the living experience he had been in, but I hoped all the letters and pictures as well as the books I had sent had kept him grounded and connected. Staying connected to family was very important, and many of the men he left behind in prison were alone. I would think about the large number of inmates and the sadness that those families had been through. We hoped and prayed that our kids would never find themselves near a prison again.

Hayden liked the halfway house where he lived but wished he could be with his friends at the other one. He did find out, however, that Pete had already moved out of the recommended halfway house because his dad had gotten him an apartment. It was completely against Burning Tree's recommendations, and they were not happy Pete had already left a support system that could have given him a better chance for sobriety. Hayden went to visit Pete and told us his new place was nice. Pete was sharing the apartment with Hayden's other friend from Burning Tree.

About two weeks passed, and Hayden was returning from work when he received a phone call from one of the guys from the other halfway house that Pete had left. Pete had overdosed on heroin and was found dead in his bed. The news was extremely upsetting for Hayden, and he called me in tears. His voice did not sound well, and I was worried about him. It broke my heart to think of Pete and his mother. She had not wanted him in the apartment yet, but she could not keep Pete's dad from getting it for him. Pete's parents were divorced and hated each other. His dad had plenty of money and gave it to Pete whenever he wanted it, which made him the enabler. I thought about how tragic this was, especially because Pete had been clean for almost two years.

Hayden and I attended the memorial service that Burning Tree hosted for Pete's family and all the residents to attend. Hayden and I rode together so we could talk. When we arrived, I knew it was going to be difficult to walk inside and see Pete's mother. Music was playing, candles were burning, and a slideshow of Pete projected on the wall. We separated as we walked in, and Hayden made his way across the room to talk to and hug people. I stopped just short of the family room and could see Pete's mother in the distance, watching the slide show in tears. I began to walk toward her, and when she saw me, she came quickly to hug me. We had met twice before, during past visitations and family weekend, which gave us a chance to get to know each other. I felt so bad for her and listened while she talked about Pete and shared stories that went along with the pictures. While we were talking, she became angry and believed maybe it was homicide and someone else injected Pete's arm, and she was still working with the police to see if they could do more. She did not want to believe he had relapsed on his own. She then began to curse about Pete's father and was disgusted with his enabling. I searched for the right words, but she was not in a place emotionally to hear me, so I put the focus back onto a photo that flashed up on the wall.

Other guests approached her to give their condolences, so I went to look around for Hayden. I watched him still making his way around the room talking to people, but I noticed he seemed a bit disconnected from the reason we were really there. He may have been in denial, not wanting to believe Pete was really gone. Everyone began to take a seat and I sat down, but Hayden stayed in the back of the room. He was struggling emotionally but continued to keep a pleasant look about him. Several of Pete's friends spoke about him during the service, but Hayden could not bring himself to do that.

The service ended, and we all went outside to form a large circle and light candles. I was standing near Hayden, but he had managed to keep his emotions in, and I so desperately wanted him to let them out and cry. A prayer was said, and the service was over. Hayden had many people he wanted to talk to before we left, and I hugged a few parents. I knew the staff at Burning Tree was sick inside to lose another one of their own, but it was their reality, and they knew the odds. Some made it and some didn't, just like with any other disease. They gave every bit of knowledge they had so Pete could help himself. It was up to the addict to use it, and if they didn't, they could lose the battle.

During our drive back to Dallas, Hayden and I talked about everything that had happened. I told Hayden I never wanted to find him like Pete and this should be a wake-up call for him.

He looked down at the floor and said, "I would never want you to find me that way either, but what if I don't make it?"

Trying not to show my alarm at what he'd said and give him support instead, I told him not think that way and reminded him that if he put his mind to it and followed his plan to stay clean, he could make it. I began to list the few friends I had that were recovering addicts and were still clean after many years. I assured him he could do it but could sense he still struggled with doubt and a lack of self-confidence.

A few days later, a call came in on my cell phone and I could tell it was Landon. I was excited.

"Landon! Where are you honey? Can we pick you up? Are you in Dallas?"

He answered with much less energy than I had and said, "Uh, no, I'm actually in Houston at another transfer unit called Luther. They are processing me in here, but it does seem to be a better place."

He was placed in the Trusty Camp, which gave him a little more freedom but it was still prison. Carl and I couldn't understand why he hadn't been released yet. He had completed his court-appointed sentence, but poor government management was holding things up. He was not told how long he would be there, so we were all very frustrated. His six-month sentence was turning into nine months, and his birthday was coming up in April. The thought of him spending another time of celebration in there made me sad, but all we could do was wait for his release.

Hayden resumed his busy schedule after dealing with the loss of Pete but was still short of completing his requirements at the halfway house. He was 95 percent complete but needed to master the last part before he could graduate there. He was not keeping up with paying his bills on time and was given several warnings, and then they took his car keys to prove a point. If you don't pay your bills, things get taken away. Hayden was furious and was told he would have to get rides to his work and meetings. Trying to manage his schedule with others who had to drive him was challenging.

After a few days, he had had enough and looked for his car keys in the office to drive himself to work. When the house director found out Hayden's actions, he felt he had no choice but to kick Hayden out of the halfway house. I got a call that afternoon from Hayden, and he told me what happened and how the director told him to pack his stuff and leave immediately. I called the director myself, and he confirmed the story to be true. He said Hayden had had more chances already than most get, and he had to leave now.

I was a bit in shock because I did not want to bring Hayden home. Carl and my past decision was he would not ever live with us again for his own good and ours. The demand happened so fast, and the only other option the director offered was for Hayden to check into the twenty-four-hour club, which was a homeless shelter for addicts. Many thoughts were going through my head, and Carl was on a plane back to Dallas so I was unable to reach him. I reminded Hayden about the plan we had and he said, "What about work and school and my probation meetings? What am I going to do?"

I told him he needed to make everything right and stay at the halfway house. He talked to the director again but was told he was out of time.

After some time passed, Hayden called me back, and I suggested maybe he should go to the twenty-four-hour club. He listed everything coming up that week, and I could hear concern in his voice. Finally, I said, "Hayden, you can stay in the guest room until we find you a place to live, but you cannot move back home."

He understood and agreed, then packed up and left the halfway house late that afternoon. This is a decision I will regret for the rest of my life because I had stepped back into enabler mode.

He arrived at our house and apologized on the way in, explaining the situation, and said the other guys did not want to give him rides everywhere and he needed his car. He felt they overreacted when they took his car keys and he had been about to take care of everything asked. He believed the director overreacted and was not fair about the situation. He moved his suitcases in, and I reminded him this was very temporary. I begin to wonder if I made the wrong decision by letting him come home. Was I the enabler now?

The decisions families face every day are extremely tough when dealing with addicts. I felt I was standing in quicksand and forced to make the "right" choice. Hayden knew what was expected, but over and over, he fell short of expectations. He would have to focus on a consistent plan, which was detrimental for success to beat his addiction. When he came into the kitchen, we started talking about his accomplishments and the fact that he was two years clean. He was so proud and said he felt great. I could sense a maturity about him and a difference in his attitude, which made me believe he was doing well. He realized he was a guest in our home and made it clear he was grateful and would respect our wishes. I reminded him how his old room had looked when he was very sick and all the destruction that I found after he left.

He said, "Yes, I was pretty messed up," but he could not remember everything that had happened.

The girls came downstairs to see him and catch up on life. Carl arrived home and spent time with us. He was surprised to see Hayden was home and asked if I remembered our plan that he would never come back home. I assured him it was temporary and I was already helping him look for apartments.

Looking for apartments was very difficult because of all the rules put in place for sex offenders. The rules were much needed for safety of children, and I could completely understand why they were established. Hayden was a teen at the time of his conviction but still had to comply with every last rule. We spent hours searching for just the right place he could move to, and it had to be approved by his probation officer. I finally found a small apartment in east Dallas about forty minutes away, but it was close to Hayden's job at a small restaurant and NA groups and school. The complex was not near any schools, churches with nurseries, playgrounds, parks, swimming pools, or daycare centers.

Talking about all of this made Hayden angry. He said, "I am not dirty, Mom. I don't even like kids or have any desire to be around them. I can't believe I have this label. I would never do any of the things I have to hear about in my sex-offense group meetings."

I, too, was still angry inside for believing that girl was Miranda's friend and the destruction she brought into our home. I knew Hayden still had some responsibility for what had happened, but her family should have handled it differently. They still lived in the same neighborhood where Hayden was arrested, on the same road I had to drive down every time I went somewhere. I would pass by and feel a tightness in my chest from the anger I felt, as the thoughts of his arrest filled my head.

We received word from the probation officer that Hayden was approved to move into the apartment complex. It was a happy day. He was thrilled and glad to be independent to start living life on his own. We began making arrangements, and then Hayden had to call the owner of the unit and explain his sex-offense charge. It was the last approval he needed to secure his spot. The owner of the unit was a young man in his thirties and completely understood Hayden's situation. The owner's best friend from high school had the same type of situation happen to him and his girlfriend. He understood it was hard to find a place to live and graciously gave Hayden the keys after all payments and paperwork were finished. We began shopping and planning for his big move.

Ten months of serving time arrived, and Landon would finally be coming home. He was able to share the location where I was to pick him up, which was an hour-and-a-half drive, or he could catch the long bus ride to Dallas. I was ready to see him, so I made the drive. The clothes he wore to his first stop in Collin County ten months earlier were the clothes he was supposed to leave in, but with all the location changes, his clothes had been lost.

When he got into the car, I asked, "What are you wearing?" He was given a very large, plaid, flannel shirt, dirty khaki pants, and black, Frankenstein-looking shoes. We hugged and laughed as he explained they lost his clothes.

We talked most of the way home, and he was looking forward to a nice, warm, private shower and toilet. He was so glad it was over and he was not going to celebrate his birthday in jail, which would be in three weeks. I got him up to date on family matters, and he was surprised Hayden was home but looked forward to seeing him. He was happy for him and glad he'd remained clean for so long and wanted to help move him into his new apartment.

We all felt like we finally had some traction and looked forward to a happy future. The girls were finishing school and eager for another vacation. We were going to Florida to enjoy the beach and Disney World. The boys were not allowed to come because of their status.

Hayden was still on probation, and Landon wasn't allowed to travel for three months after his release. Before our trip, we had a lot to do, with Hayden moving out and into his apartment and Miranda graduating high school. Out-of-town family came down to support Miranda, and she was happy and ready to move on to college.

Weeks passed, and summer arrived. Landon was spending all of his time working on an engineering project and was glad to be home. He was deciding his next move and the direction he felt best for his future. He was having a hard time sleeping soundly because of the nightmares he was experiencing about being back in prison. His dreams put him back in the cold cell, just waiting to be released again. These dreams lasted for a long time. He and Hayden would see each other in passing because Hayden was coming and going with his busy schedule.

It was time for another probation meeting. When Hayden arrived back home, he was very distraught because he was informed he had to spend three weeks in jail for the past polygraph test. The DA would not waive the punishment. Even though he had been in two years of recovery and therapy, she said this had nothing to do with his sex-offense charge. Hayden couldn't believe it. The memories of his jaw getting broken in there made him cringe. None of us could do anything but give Hayden encouragement and remind him how short his stay would be. He was assigned a day to check in.

I assured him we would finish his apartment and get him all moved in, and that is where he could go when he got out to start a fresh, new life. He was happy to hear that, and it made checking himself into Collin County much easier. He got to go with me on one supply-shopping and pick out his kitchen needs before he went to jail. I continued looking for furniture bargains and artwork for the wall to get his apartment furnished and give it a homey feel. His apartment had two small bedrooms, and he was planning on finding a roommate, but, until then, one room would be his music-engineering studio and the other his bedroom. I found a great deal on a contemporary bedroom suite and some artwork with guitars and quotes about the love of music. It took some fast planning to make sure the place was ready for him when he was released from jail. The girls and I were also finalizing our vacation plans. Landon would stay at the house to take care of the place, and Hayden would be in his new home in Dallas.

Hayden checked into jail, which he said would absolutely be his last time. He said to us with a casual laugh, "You know I would rather be dead than spend my life in jail." He was ready to get it over and felt smart enough to handle it this time. He decided to have a good attitude and do what he could in there to pass time. Miranda felt bad for him, and I could tell she had thoughts about the past but knew she could not make herself responsible.

Three weeks passed and Hayden was released to go home. He came by our house to get a quick shower and pack up the last of his things. We went to lunch and then by the grocery store before arriving at his apartment. As we pulled in, he had a big smile on his face and said, "I'm finally doing this, a place of my own."

We went in, he looked around, and he loved the décor. He said, "Nice job, Mom." He went to the kitchen to put away his food and organize his utensils and cooking supplies. I didn't finish everything because I felt it was important for him to decide where his goods should be. After he finished with that, he started his favorite part, setting up his music-recording area in the extra bedroom. He had plans to start a new song and explained the sound-layering process. Before I left, we discussed the importance of keeping everything clean and made sure he felt comfortable with all the appliances. He said, "Mom, I learned all this at Burning Tree. I got this. I know how to clean." I laughed and agreed. We hugged good-bye, and I headed home.

Before we left for Florida, we met with Hayden a few times. On one occasion, Landon and I took lunch to Hayden and sat at his new little kitchen table that had two chairs. I grabbed a box that had not been sent to recycling yet and sat on that. Halfway through lunch, it collapsed with me on it and the boys had a good laugh. As lunch was finishing up, Hayden began to rush us out and said he would take care of the dishes, and it was so good to see us. I just assumed he wanted to take responsibility and do it on his own, so we left. A small part of me felt a little concern, but I didn't want to overreact.

The Fourth of July was near and we were leaving for Florida on the fifth, so we made plans to meet Hayden for dinner. The girls decided not to go because they were packing and hanging out with friends. Landon joined us to see Hayden and visit. We arrived on the time planned, but Hayden was late as usual. He came to the table, sat down, and he and Landon struck up conversation, but Hayden seemed a little uncomfortable. He was with us but not connected, and his eyes seemed to watch everyone around us, which meant it took forever for him to decide what he wanted to eat. I asked if he felt okay, and he said, "Yes, for sure," then made a joke to lighten us up. He said he was looking forward to meeting up with his friends from the halfway house to shoot fireworks later that evening. He asked if we could give him some extra money for fireworks, so we gave him some cash. We finished dinner, and he and Landon got up to walk around before dessert came.

Carl looked at me and said, "Do you think Hayden is acting a little weird?"

I said yes, and we both felt concerned. Carl decided to have a heart-to-heart talk with him because we were flying out the next day to Florida. After dessert, Landon and I walked slowly to give Carl and Hayden plenty of time to walk ahead and talk. Hayden assured Carl he was fine and staying clean. He reminded Carl about his meetings and his mentor. Carl offered not to leave for Florida if Hayden needed him and asked him to be completely honest.

Hayden laughed and said, "Dad, I'm fine. You are not missing your trip! I'll stay in touch with you while you're gone, and I have plenty to do here."

Landon and I approached them as they were hugging and Carl was telling Hayden he was proud of him for staying clean. I gave Hayden a big hug and kiss and said, "I'll call you tomorrow."

The boys fist-bumped, and Hayden told Landon, "Stay cool, bro."

The next morning, Carl and the girls and I caught our flight to Florida. The girls laughed and talked the whole flight. The vacation had finally arrived, and they were full of energy. They spent an hour looking at the rides and activities we could not miss at Disney World and Universal Studios. A brand-new area was based on Harry Potter and would be open for the first time the weekend we arrived. Carl had a business connection with one of the Universal Studios executives, so we received VIP passes, which granted us easy access throughout the entire park. We were able to bypass the crowd and ride anything twice. The girls were in heaven. We had a three-day pass, and then we were going to drive to the beach.

During our three days at Disney and Universal Studios, I heard from Hayden several times and he told me about his new beat. Sometimes he sounded agitated, but he said he really needed some speakers we had at our house. I told him they might be in the attic and that I would look when I get home. He said, "Okay, but I really need them."

A few more days passed, and our vacation was coming to an end. Landon let me know the house was kept clean and all was well there. I called Hayden the evening before we left Florida to check in with him, and he was glad we were coming home. He reminded me again about the speakers and said we were going to love his new music. He really wanted us to come down and hear it. I told him we would love to and would see him tomorrow.

Late morning arrived, and we drove to turn in our rental car and catch our flight. We were returning on Carl and my twenty-eighth wedding anniversary and had plans later that evening to celebrate. I texted Hayden to let him know what time we landed but did not get a response. We landed at DFW airport that afternoon and drove home to see Landon. Evening was setting in, and I still had not heard from Hayden. We did not know his schedule so assumed he could be at work or an NA meeting. I emptied a few suitcases, called him again, and did not get an answer. Carl and I decided to visit him and check in. I grabbed the speakers out of the attic, and we headed to his apartment.

—12—

Funeral

As we approached the small apartment complex on July 11, 2014 in southeast Dallas, we could see Hayden's black Elantra parked out front. Just three weeks earlier, we'd helped move him into his apartment and decorate the place to feel like home. It had been a long search to find the right spot for him, and he was so excited to finally be living on his own. He was back in school and working part-time, which was a huge feat for him due to all of his circumstances.

It was getting dark outside, and night was approaching. My heart began to pick up its pace because I was nervous as we climbed to the second floor and began knocking on his door. I was hoping he would throw the door open and give us his big smile and make some funny joke as he usually would. After a minute passed, we let ourselves in with the extra key and called out his name.

"Hayden, we're here." We quickly scanned the room, looking for him. We stood in his front living room and could see the kitchen light was on, but all was silent. His opened boxes of food in the distance were sitting on the counter, and a few articles of clothing were lying around. Silence was the first clue that something was wrong. Hayden always had music, TV, or a video game playing. It was not like him to be in silence. His passion was audio engineering, and he spent hours trying to make that just-right beat and sound for others to enjoy. Carl told me to stay in the living room and he would head to the bedroom to look for him. He walked around the corner to find our son lying on the side of his bed. A few seconds passed and Carl quickly came back around the corner, grasped me tight, and let me know Hayden was dead. I screamed and fell to the floor in agony and disbelief. Carl came to my side, hugging me, and told me I would not want to see Hayden that way because signs showed he had been lying there for many hours. He quickly called 911 and then sat beside me as he cried out. Our hearts were broken, and I felt as if a part of me had died.

The last conversation I had with Hayden was the evening before and he had been waiting for us to get back from vacation. We sat in Hayden's lifeless apartment and my face was still buried in my hands and I could not find my composure, the tears still streaming down my face, and Carl, beside me, trying to be strong. We could hear the sounds of sirens in the distance as they broke the silence and approached with lights flashing. The sound of quick footsteps came up the stairs, and I just could not believe this was happening to us.

I sat, paralyzed, as Carl got up to answer the door. All I could do was look at the floor in between the floods of tears. Two officers came in and gave their condolences. In a soft voice, one officer began asking Carl a list of questions. He was answering the best he could and informed them our son was a recovering addict. I knew we would have to call our other three kids and share the awful news. They all loved Hayden dearly despite the last eight difficult years.

The police and investigators filled the apartment and began to search for clues to rule out homicide. Carl continued to answer all of the questions because I could not speak. For the first time in my life, I was without a voice. I had never known real despair or the feeling of emptiness. I had seen images of situations like this on TV or in the movies but never thought this would be a part of my life. The emotion

I was feeling was very foreign to me because I had never lost anyone close to me. I felt as if I had been hit with a sledgehammer and could not think straight. I was sitting just around the corner from my dead son, who I would never see again on earth. With my eyes shut tight, I could see his smiling face, and in my head, I could hear his voice. All I had of my child was memories now. I would have to cling to the wonderful ones and deal with the ones that made me hurt for him. He had finally lost his battle. An awful, dark journey he had been on for eight years.

It was time to make the call to our other three kids, and I was still speechless. Carl made the calls, and the kids waited at our home until we could return later that evening. I knew I had to pull myself together for them. They had seen us fight Hayden's drug addiction for years, which was like being in battle every day. I had remained strong to keep the rest of us going as if we were living in a different reality apart from Hayden's. For us, it was like two lives. Now the realities collided and we lost our beloved Hayden, at the age of twenty-two.

The investigators were finishing up and the ambulance had arrived to remove Hayden's corpse from his room. They let us know they found heroin on the counter, but they would send him in for an autopsy. They said he most likely died from an accidental heroin overdose. When we heard the news, it made sense that this could be his cause of death, but what did not make sense was why, after two years clean, he used drugs again. That is the hardest question to answer, especially when the one you love tells you he wants to stay clean but relapses.

Carl and I left the sad apartment to wait in our car so we would not have to experience our child's exit. As we sat in silence, I turned to look over my shoulder and through the darkness, and I could see the stretcher and Hayden's silhouette under the sheet that was his temporary tomb. I was still in disbelief, and the tears began to fall upon my face again. We waited until the ambulance had left, and, with breaking hearts, we closed up his silent apartment.

The thirty-minute drive home felt long as I started to prepare myself for the grim sadness that awaited us at our home. When we arrived, Landon was sitting emotionless at the kitchen table with a look of disbelief on his face. He was speechless because he had just been getting to know Hayden again and believed he was going to be okay. As I hugged him, I could hear the girls crying and clinging to each other. I turned toward them, and their faces were red and wet.

The first words out of Miranda's mouth were, "It's my fault, and I feel so guilty!" The past was stirring her emotions to feel responsible. She knew the stress Hayden had felt from his sex-offense charge. I took them in my arms and assured her it was not her fault. We all dropped to the floor, and I knew I had to be strong for them. We sat there for an hour trying to process everything that had happened. Landon stayed silent, and I believe he was still in disbelief. The brother he was starting to bond with again was gone.

Trying to sleep that night was extremely difficult, and I wanted to disconnect from reality. Not only would this date be remembered as the day Hayden passed away but also Carl and my twenty-eighth year wedding anniversary. It was very ironic and really unbelievable that such a joy and such a tragedy could share the same day. I remember Carl whispering to me after we finally lay down in bed and it was quiet and dark. He said, "Honey, we lost Hayden on our anniversary." I lay there, silent, as tears began to drip from my eyes onto my pillow. I just wanted to sleep and not think. The next morning when I opened my eyes, the tears began to fall again, and I felt empty. I could see Hayden's smiling, sober face and hear his laughter in my head.

We were all still in shock, and the next few days would be very hard as we had to notify the family to plan his funeral. My sister Rene and her family were on a cruise, and she was the first one I needed to call. I was sick inside and knew they would be sad and shocked to hear the unexpected news. Our kids were close growing up and spent many fun times together, and they were very supportive all the years we struggled with our family issues and Hayden's addiction. I didn't want to tell my mom and dad without family support in town for them. My dad had suffered a heart attack several years before, and I didn't want to take any chances at causing him another.

Carl made calls to his family, and I called other family and friends to share our heartbreaking news. The words "we lost Hayden" were the hardest words ever to come out of our mouths. It was taking a few days to find where my sister was, so I decided to call my parents' neighbors and have them on-call if my parents needed comfort when I shared our tragic news. My parents helped raise Hayden when he was young, while I was in college. They were a big part of his life and were saddened when they found out he was addicted to drugs. They prayed daily for him and are people of strong faith. It was time to make the call to them, and the second my mom heard my voice, she knew something was wrong. I immediately began to cry and tell her Hayden was gone. She didn't understand at first, and I shared the details. We talked awhile and she told me, as her tears began to fall, that she would go tell my dad. She believed he would be okay but said she would contact her neighbors if they needed help. I let her know I was still trying to reach Rene and hoped to soon. Rene finally received my message to call her because of an emergency. When she heard the news, she was sick inside and dreaded telling the rest of the family. The ship was docking the next morning, and they were given emergency leave and allowed to exit the ship first. She knew I was a mess and would need the strength of the family, so they were planning to get to us as soon as possible.

Carl brought me and the kids together in the living room to discuss how we wanted to put together Hayden's funeral. We all agreed we wanted to do it in a way that would make Hayden proud, and music was a passion of his, so finding all the right music to play was very important. We reached out to our church and met with one of our younger pastors, who understood Hayden's battle with addiction and who we felt was perfect to deliver the spiritual message. We had the kids help us find pictures of Hayden to play at the reception because we felt it was very important that we, as a family, arranged this funeral together. I knew with Landon just returning from prison, the blow of this tragedy was extremely difficult for him, but he was trying to be helpful. Carl was strong and trying to manage some of the other arrangements, and the two of us would go to the funeral home and decide on coffins or vases, depending on how we would bury Hayden. We took a favorite picture of Hayden that would be copied to the front of his funeral announcement. My sister and brother-in-law arrived in time to go with us. I was not sure I could make it through the meeting, so their support was much-appreciated. It just did not seem real that we were planning one of our own's funeral.

I knew in my heart that Hayden would be mad at himself for doing this to the family, and I knew he had so much he still wanted to say to each of us. We had that discussion months earlier that I never wanted to find him the way we did, and he agreed. We finished our selections at the Sparkman Funeral Home and decided to cremate Hayden. I was still struggling with that choice and needed a little more time to think. The thought of turning my son to ashes was tearing me up inside. I decided to go for a run to help clear my head and relieve some anxiety. I had music playing that reminded me about the spirit leaving a broken dwelling place, and I knew then that Hayden was finally free of the broken body he was trying to survive in. His soul was at peace, and he would never feel the pain, confusion, and suffering from his disease again. His body was just a place, and he had left it. I turned toward home to talk with Carl and confirm our decision. I explained my thoughts to the kids, and they agreed as well. Miranda and Olivia were sitting at the dining room table looking through old pictures, which brought tears to us all. They were choosing them for the slide show of Hayden that Carl was creating. I went to sit outside to collect my thoughts and process what all we were dealing with. I decided I needed to write a letter to Carl and the kids as if Hayden had written it and read it to them at the funeral to help us find closure. Hayden and I were so close, and he'd told me his feelings many times in the past, which would help me write this letter. I prayed about it and asked God to give me the strength to find the right words. I explained to Carl what I felt I needed to do, and he also wanted to speak at the funeral in hopes of sending a message about addiction.

Hayden's friends from the halfway house were going to be his pallbearers and sit on the front row. Carl and I knew it would be difficult to speak with Hayden lying just below us. I continued to pray we would find strength. All of us posted the "In Loving Memory" memorial announcement on Facebook along with a beautiful message about Hayden. Despite his struggles for years, he was loved by so many who knew him in the past, as well as us. Many supporting messages began to pour in and touch our hearts. Carl and I finished our messages to read at the funeral, but I told him I wanted him to hear mine for the first time when I read it at the service. We finished up the music selection and pictures. It was very hard to sleep before the memorial service the next day.

Dawn broke and the sun was going to shine today, which helped the mood. The girls and I dressed in black and wanted to look nice for Hayden. He loved when we all dressed up, and he, too, enjoyed looking nice, so this would be done for him. Landon was quiet but present. Carl hugged me to make sure I was okay. Both sides of our family arrived—aunts, uncles, cousins, and grandparents. We loaded up in the black stretch limos to ride to Sparkman's chapel, where the memorial service would be delivered. We arrived early for some quiet time in the chapel before others arrived. Beautiful flower arrangements were everywhere, filling the entry and throughout the chapel. We made our way down front to sit and wait for Hayden to be brought in. Tears poured down my face, and Carl reached for my hand. The girls, too, were very emotional and Landon sat, staring ahead. The rest of the family filed in behind us, and the soft music with touching lyrics began to play. This was the music that was handpicked by all of us on Hayden's behalf. The pallbearers slowly came in, carrying Hayden with tears in their eyes. He was placed in front of us, and his casket opened. That vision will forever remain in my mind. It was just surreal to see his body lying there but with no spark at all. We all stood up together to walk toward the casket and say our good-byes. I reached out and gently touched him one last time. We took our seats, and friends began pouring in to hug us and see Hayden. Their support and love filled the entire chapel. We had two hundred guests that day, and I knew Hayden would have been so touched to see so much love and support.

The service started, and I hoped I would be able to make it through the letter I was going to read. In my head, I practiced it several times, imagining myself standing over Hayden. It was important to me to do this for the family. My time had come, and I climbed the stairs up to the podium. I looked out into the loving faces that came that day and then at the kids and Carl. I leaned toward the microphone and explained why I wrote this for Hayden and that it was written as if he had written it. This is the letter I wrote and read.

HAYDEN'S FAREWELL LETTER

I want to say thank you to all of you who have come today to support my family. I love my family very much, and I am sorry to be gone. I will miss the good times, the laughter, the great family vacations, and the big family gatherings for the holidays. I will miss making all the awesome tracks and beats I know I was going to compose and share with the world. There are many things that I will miss, but I am so glad to finally be at peace. Life has been a struggle for me for the past eight years. My disease of addiction was very difficult for me to handle, and I wish I had reached out more. I know you guys were there for me. You made sure I had the best care and support, and I do appreciate that. I want to speak to each of you, my closest family members, directly because I had more to say to you and shared these things with Mom.

Landon, my bro. I am so glad I got to spend time with you right before I left, dude. We have been so distant for the past six years and I am responsible for that, but getting to spend the couple of weeks I did with you and seeing the awesome project you are working on made me so proud of you. I always knew you were very smart and would do something awesome someday. Sorry for all the hard times I gave you as a kid and all the names I called you, which we won't mention now. I love you, brother. Good luck.

Hey, Miranda, what's up? You look awesome in that black dress. I'm so glad we shared so many good times, and you hold a special place in my heart. You did nothing wrong to cause this, and I am sorry for the pain I have caused you these past several years. I am so proud of you and know your future will be amazing. Can't wait to see the trippin' outfits you will design for the world to see. So glad you got it together, girl. I love you.

Hey, Olivia. Wow, look how tall you are, girl. I hear you are an awesome volleyball player and really smart. That's really cool. I know you want to be called Doctor someday. Good luck with that. I wanted to spend more time with you. I am sorry for the confusion you must have felt so often when I was struggling. I want you to remember me as your funny brother. I loved hearing you laugh. You are a sweet girl, and please stay that way. I love you.

Hey, Dad. I should have listened to you more; you had so much you wanted to share with me and gave me the best advice, but I was stubborn and didn't listen to you. I am so sorry and wish I had listened more. I admire you so much and wanted to walk in those business shoes of yours. You amaze me with everything you can do. I wanted to be there and watch your new businesses grow. Thanks for all the great trips and awesome gourmet food we ate. I enjoyed seeing you cook in the kitchen and always knew it was going to be something delicious. You are a great Dad and my hero. Proud to have you as my Dad.

Hey, Mom. I can't believe I did this. I am so sorry. You told me you never wanted to find me this way. Just know that it is so peaceful now. Don't worry about me. You were there for me every step of the way and are an awesome mom. You're the best. I am so glad we were so close and laughed so much. You listened to all my stories and dreams. I know you would have given your life for me. I love you so much, and I am glad you have Landon, Miranda, Olivia, and Dad there by your side. Keep being the happy person that you are and enjoy life, Mom. I am waiting for you all in heaven.

I want everyone to know that I was sharing in Bible study and prayer group with two friends of mine and let Jesus into my heart a few months back and was hoping to be baptized. Thank you to my friends who were helping me change my life and giving me so much encouragement.

To all of my homies and any of you struggling with addiction, reach out for help. Please don't wait when you have those weak moments. Use the tools you have to help you be strong. Especially your higher power. Let my death mentor to you and be an example to help you so that you can move on and live a full, happy life. Keep enjoying the rhythm of life, and never take for granted the beat of your heart. Catch y'all later.

I was weak in the knees as I read the letter and noticed the guys from the halfway house crying on the front row. I knew they must have been thinking it could have been one of them. The kids and Carl were wiping away their tears but were able to smile some as I looked into their eyes while reading to each of them. I was glad I was able to finish Hayden's letter in hopes of comforting the family and maybe help anyone in the crowd who might be struggling. I finished and turned to walk down the stairs as Carl was coming up to speak to the crowd, and he hugged me while saying, "That was beautiful, honey."

I took my seat between the kids to hold hands as we looked up at Carl, now standing above Hayden's casket. We all shed more tears as he shared nice memories of Hayden then spoke on the subject of addiction. Carl spoke well, and we both wanted to share words of encouragement to anyone there who needed them. Many tears and heavy emotions filled the room as we sat quietly listening to the song "Coming Home."

The service came to an end, and we gathered for a reception and Hayden's picture slide show. Everyone gathered around as we watched our beautiful son's baby pictures and all the others throughout his life. My chest was tight as the memories seemed to swell inside my battered heart. We knew he was gone, but he would never be forgotten. Friends and family formed a line to hug us and tell us how much they loved Hayden. His old friends from Highland Park High School came and wanted to share the funny stories and great memories they had of him. Many of them had graduated college and had no idea Hayden had been struggling for so long. The news came as a shock to them. Friends from Burning Tree and a few staff that worked with Hayden also came that day in support of our family. It hurt every time one of their own did not make it. The gathering was coming to an end, so our family filled the cars to take us home again.

On our departure, the funeral program director asked if they should bring Hayden's flowers out to the house. Because I did not have a chance to really see them, I said yes, please. The next day the flowers came and, to our surprise, sixty different large arrangements were brought in, and they were amazing. We had no idea there were so many. All of the out-of-town family came for dinner, and we walked around, admiring the flowers. This helped take my mind off of the funeral for a while. Our family sat around that evening, outside on our back patio, and we shared stories. The nights were hard for me. Something about the darkness made me sad and long for morning. Most of the family left the next day to resume life. Times like these make everyone realize how precious life is and how important family and friends are.

Several days passed, and it was time to go back to Hayden's lifeless apartment. This would be my first time to return, and I knew it would be very difficult. Carl had to attend a court case out of town and could not go with me. Landon graciously came instead to help me clean, sort, and pack up before the movers could come to pack furniture. It seemed so wrong that we had just moved Hayden in and now were moving out. We arrived and walked in, and the pain of the memories finding Hayden in a passing state hurt. I took a few minutes to get my emotions under control. Landon and I worked and loaded as much as we could into my car and the Elantra that Landon would drive home. As we boxed up items, I thought about Hayden and the last time I was at his apartment, with him playing music for us.

I returned to the apartment the next day to meet with the moving company, who took the rest of the boxes and furniture to a small storage unit I rented. When they were finished, I stood in the middle of the empty apartment and cried for a while. As I was leaving, a middle-aged woman, who lived a few units away from Hayden, approached me. She knew he must have passed from all of the activity that night when the police and ambulance came. She gave me her condolences and said she had met Hayden and that he was so kind to her and the other residents when they would see him outside. I knew she wondered what happened to him, so I shared a brief history to help her understand. It made her sad to hear about his battle against drug addiction. She said would have never guessed that about him. I hugged her and thanked her for the kind words, and she wished me well.

As I drove away, I felt a strong need to talk to Hayden and wished he could hear me. I began to cry from the pain and heartbreak as I talked to him out loud anyway because it helped me feel better. I began to realize why people believe their loved one's spirit must still be around. There is such a need to talk to them that you look around for clues that their spirit might be present. It is very hard to let go of them, even when the burial is over, because many believe the spirit is set free to roam. It was a beautiful thought, so I chose to believe Hayden's spirit was happy in the sky with the angels, playing music in the heavens for God. God created Hayden, but the manmade elements on earth distorted him, so God took him home to ease his pain.

I remembered that I prayed to God that He would help our son find peace, so He must have seen this as the only way for Hayden after the long battle. I thought back to the time when the family went to visit Hayden at Burning Tree and what a beautiful weekend that was. He was clear-headed and apologized to the kids, Carl, and me for all the hurt he caused the family the past years and wished his life had unfolded differently. He shared encouraging words and let us all know how much he loved us and appreciated the support we'd given him. I was so glad we were able to hear that from him and it still held a special place in my wounded heart. I knew we would all have to cling to the wonderful times we had with Hayden to help us heal. I arrived home and Olivia greeted me at the door with her beautiful smile and a big hug.

—13—

Healing Hearts

He heals the brokenhearted and binds up their wounds.
—PSALM 147:3

The next several months after losing Hayden were very difficult and confusing. I did not feel complete, and every day brought tears to my eyes when I thought of him because the memories of him were beautiful and painful at the same time. The hardest part of the day was lying down at night to sleep when the house was quiet, and I began to dread nighttime because the darkness outside brought with it a deep sadness. I would try to pray but was no longer sure if God was real. I struggled with thoughts of creation and why Hayden's life became as it did. He would never experience the many joys of life, such as graduating college, having a career, getting married to the girl of his dreams, and having a family of his own. My faith had been shaken, and for the first time in my life, I felt doubt, which made me feel guilty. My faith in God was what kept me strong for those long, hard eight years, but now I found myself with a different perspective. I was on the "other side" of life because I'd experienced such a tragic loss.

We were all changed emotionally and mentally from trying to understand how this tragedy was now a part of our lives. Each of us would struggle in our own way from the pain and heartache. My head was filled with the question "why us?" but I began to remember my prayer years earlier when I asked God to help our boys find peace in their lives. Was Hayden's passing his peace and ours?

The one thing we all agreed on was that Hayden was now resting in peace, and this comment was made many times at his funeral by us and by others. I knew with time and healing wounds, peace would return to us as a family and my spirit would find peace with God.

All of us seemed battered emotionally, but each of us handled the hurt in different ways. Olivia began to ask more questions, with hopes to find some kind of understanding about Hayden's drug use and why he had the disease. Her questions were hard to answer, but I knew she needed to hear as much as I knew about his condition and the horrible dangers of experimenting with drugs. She had seen and heard Hayden at his worst, which helped her understand everything we'd talked about.

Miranda was fragile and struggled emotionally with thoughts of the past because she still held onto the past and some guilt about how she may have affected Hayden. She adored him and would forever miss the relationship they could have continued. When they were young, they talked about him being Uncle Hayden some day and laughed at the sound of that title. She knew she would cherish the great memories and stories about him.

Landon hid his emotions and did not say much. He absorbed himself in projects and one in particular that consumed him the most. When he and I cleaned out Hayden's apartment, we brought all his music equipment home, as well as his laptop, which was full of recordings of him rapping when he was younger, as well as his last audio-engineering production in progress. None of us knew Hayden's laptop password, so Landon was determined to hack into it in hopes of retrieving a part of Hayden. After several days, Landon had success and called Carl and me upstairs to listen to Hayden's last song. Our emotions were stirred as we listened to the music Hayden was working on the day he passed away. I lay down on the floor and closed my eyes to picture him at his desk, creating his masterpiece. He wanted the speakers I was bringing to hear his music surround sound. Tears began to fall as I asked Landon to play it again. We could hear the song was not quite finished, so Landon decided he would learn how to use the equipment and finish it for his brother. We liked the idea and felt this was Landon's way of dealing with the loss.

Carl was my comfort and my strength, but it was time for him to get back to work just a few days after losing Hayden. I knew that was how he wanted to deal with the loss. He could lose himself in his work and stay occupied, away from the sad feelings, and, in a way, I envied that a little bit. I spent a lot of time outside gardening and taking care of the livestock. Inside the house, I had to have noise such as the television or music to keep my mind from wandering into the darkness and feeling depressed. I did not want to be on any prescription medication, so I found other ways to deal with the pain. I spent time thinking about the rest of the family and how blessed we were to have each other. I still had three beautiful kids who I loved dearly, a good husband, and plenty of family and friends. Being positive and looking for the beautiful things in life would help our hearts heal, so I began to put focus on the family and keep our communication strong.

As the months passed, writing songs and poems became therapeutic for me. Besides talking and sharing verbally, releasing feelings onto paper brought me comfort. I began to spend several hours a day in the home office writing about Hayden and his struggles, as well as Carl and my family plans that were interrupted by a dark disease. Ironically, Landon was upstairs doing the same type of therapy through music. He finished Hayden's last song and titled it "Why." When I listened to it for the first time, it gave me chills from the beats of the different instruments Hayden created and sound effects Landon added. He also inserted a deep voice in a loud whisper, saying "why" repeatedly. The work and additions he added to the existing sound made perfect sense, and I told him Hayden would be proud of him. Landon continued to create his own music and also write lyrics. He didn't want to talk about the loss of his brother but began to express himself through writing.

After I wrote poems, I would let the family read them. Here are a few I wrote the first year after losing Hayden.

HEAL TOGETHER

We met, became high school sweethearts many years ago.
You took my hand and I took yours, it was meant to be, I know.
Started planning for our future, soon wedding bells did ring.
The preacher pronounced us married, and the angels started to sing.
Baby after baby, our family really grew.
We learned along the way, not always knowing what to do.
The little hands, the little feet, in amazement, we watched grow.
We turned around and they were grown, where did the time go?
But life has unexpected turns that no one can prepare.
Losing your firstborn child is oh, so hard to bear.
We looked into each other's eyes with so much disbelief.
We knew being together though would get us through the grief.

It seems like the pain will last forever,
but we can get through it if we heal together.
The sadness we feel will not last forever
because we can get through this if we heal together,

So I'll take your hand, and you take mine,
and we will heal together till the end of time.

The days pass by and the memories cause pain.
We miss him so much and life's just not the same.
Our hearts are heavy and some days it's hard to bare.
No matter where we go, we feel him everywhere.
We hear his laugh and see his smiling face,
But we draw comfort knowing he's in a better place.
God is with him and the angels sing,
The same ones that did when our wedding bells ring.
So life goes on and we rely on each other.
We can make it through it all if we have one another.

It seems like the pain will last forever,
but we can get through it if we heal together.
The sadness we feel will not last forever
because we can get through this if we heal together,
So I'll take your hand, and you take mine,
and we will heal together till the end of time.

This poem came to me as I thought about how important Carl and my strong relationship helped during the past years. I felt blessed that we had stood by each other and worked together for the good of the family. I also began praying for strong faith again and pictured Hayden being taken care of by angels. His bright spirit was in complete peace since leaving his broken body. These thoughts led me to the next poem.

THE ANGELS CALLED YOU HOME

Shadow of uncertainty always followed you.
Living in your own world, the only one you knew.
Your big imagination, the fear in your eyes
Would always find some way to put you in disguise.
You felt the world around you was always so unfair.
You struggled with the fact that anyone really cared.
No matter how much I loved you, I could not fix your pain.
You now have gone before me but I know it's Heaven's gain.

You no longer feel alone because the angels called you home.
As you walk up in the clouds, the heavens you will roam,
Feeling happy, feeling free from your anxiety,
You no longer feel alone because the angels called you home.

Good memories I will have of you from the short time we shared.
You could make me laugh and you made me cry,
but I know you really cared.
The troubles you were facing made life hard to understand.
I wish you had reached out more when I offered you my hand.
The pride you felt, the sadness you carried
Put weight on your shoulders till the day you were buried.

You no longer feel alone because the angels called you home.
As you walk up in the clouds, the heavens you will roam.
Feeling happy, feeling free from your anxiety,
You no longer feel alone because the angels called you home.

Save a place for me, please, save a place for me.
Someday we'll be together for all eternity.

Not a single day has passed that I haven't thought about Hayden. Our family motto for him became "Gone but never forgotten." I won't ever forget the joy and laughter he brought so many when he was well, and this helps my healing process. He was able to have an impact on other drug abusers when he was clean. While living at the halfway house, Hayden had the opportunity to speak to a large group at the twenty-four-hour club for addicts one evening in Dallas, encouraging them to live clean for a better chance in life. Even though he did not make it, he could have helped someone else just by saying those words, and if one person was helped then he had success. He did not want anyone to be sick like him.

Even though Hayden left us, his humor is still here and makes us laugh as we remember the great times we shared with him. Hayden would want only the best for us, and he would rather us laugh about him than mourn for him. Some days, the way our lives changed still does not seem real, but time continues to heal us, and we still love Hayden with all of our scarred hearts.

—14—

Path to Peace

Through writing poems and songs, I began to think about other families, parents, and kids who could face troubles like ours. There are already so many people being affected by drug abuse and addiction. Heroin abuse is at an all-time high and so is death from drug overdose and opioid abuse. Many like us had no idea that sadness and grief would creep into their homes, and the families that would talk at rehab shared many similarities to our family. Everyone felt very unaware, uneducated, and many times, in denial about the situation unfolding with their loved one.

The subject of drug abuse is too silent, and many are too ashamed to discuss it openly. I think about all the years my kids heard "just say no" during drug-awareness week (also called Red Ribbon Week) at school and did not really understand what they were saying no to. The schools were having door-decorating contests and daily dress-up for fun to represent the horrible dangers of drugs. But I began to think something was very wrong with this approach. Kids were seeing drug-awareness week as something fun because of the way it was being presented to them. They weren't being informed how dark, ugly, and deadly drugs were. Many had no idea what drug paraphernalia even looked like, and there was a clear lack of education around prevention.

Like all other deadly diseases, preventative care is needed, and parents have to be educated on early detection. In addition to all of this, parents and kids need to be educated on legal issues on and off school campuses. Because both of our boys encountered different kind of legal issues that cost them many hours in jail and us thousands of dollars, I see a great need to improve how society presents drug and legal awareness to our youth. The more they know, the better they can grow.

Many times, people are afraid to talk about serious matters because they feel if they bring it up, it could make someone want to do it. I haven't found this to be true. A very good example is when I finally decided our daughter Olivia needed to hear about Miranda cutting herself and all I learned about it. Olivia asked me many questions and sat thinking for a while. Some time passed before we discussed it again, but when we did, she announced there was no way she could ever do that to herself. She loved Miranda dearly and was glad she quit hurting herself. This understanding actually helped Olivia deal with a friend of her own, who talked of cutting herself and was struggling emotionally. We were able to reach out to her friend's parents and inform them what was being said by their daughter and how we understood this matter. Olivia is still friends with her to this day, and she is doing well. I am very glad that our family has become very open to discuss all matters.

As time has passed, my heart has become passionate about helping others feel comfortable discussing situations like we experienced. I think about the dreams I had and believe somehow my subconscious knew Hayden was at risk for being overtaken by something, but at the time, I didn't know how to make sense of it all. The visions of him in danger were as clear today as they were when I first dreamt them. I tried to suppress those images but couldn't. Families should not have to live through the pain of addiction, but if this does enter their lives, they need to be better educated to handle the crisis. Communities need to come together in support of open discussion about drug use, mental health, and legal issues. We have to put away shame for this crisis to get better. I know the embarrassment we felt because it was a silent subject. I do believe this epidemic is finally being recognized by the public and even by politicians, which is a huge first step. As we all know, the first step is to admit there is a problem and talk about it for a greater chance of success.

I feel angry knowing most illegal drugs come in through the Mexico border because of its openness. Hayden bought nasty stuff that took his life because it was so easy to purchase. When he was clean, he told me he only had to go several miles away to get his fix, and dealers were easy to find. There is an overabundance of drugs, which also drives the price down as it pours in across our borders. We have lived the nightmare, which keeps this from being a political situation for us and makes it a life-or-death one. If drugs were much harder to get to, Hayden might still be alive today. This is also true for addictive medications prescribed by doctors. Many times, pain medication (opioids) and anti-anxiety medications (such as Xanax) are very easy to get from a medical professional who should know to limit use and possibly not even prescribe them at all. There is a need for tighter regulations on controlled substances. Addictive medications are titled "controlled substances" for a reason, and many doctors and pharmaceutical companies are failing to control them and making more money off the prescriptions. Everyone needs to understand for the good of themselves and their families that being over-medicated with addictive drugs to take away physical pain or mental pain has great consequences. There is a balance and other treatment options to be considered, such as non-addictive medications and counseling.

We are like time capsules holding memories of the past; some are wonderful and others are painful. Like opening a capsule, if we talk and share what we are holding inside, others can learn from us and our experiences. Hope can be spread when we open our hearts to others, listen to their stories, and share ours. Several years and many holidays have passed since Hayden left us. Our wounds are becoming scars and our hearts have been healing, but, like all scars, they are reminders of the past. Scars never go away but do fade and are easier to talk about with time.

I began sharing our story with friends and strangers with hopes of helping somehow, and, time and time again, many others were able to share with me concerns and fears they had for a loved one. Many lives have been touched by addiction in many ways, and people need support, while many kids feel the pressures to try substances and drugs or need an "out." I cannot be silent knowing how disruptive and deadly drugs are, therefore I believe all families need to have a plan to learn and discuss all aspects of drug abuse. It is time for more than "just say no." Many kids might not have the addictive genetic trait but find themselves in legal trouble because they are around drugs or alcohol and wish they had a way out. Most kids want to be accepted and not made fun of and therefore stay with the crowd. How amazing it will be when the day comes that the "crowd" is large, drug free, and can help those struggling with addiction. When we can convince kids through education, pictures, and information that drugs are awful and very deadly, lives can be saved.

I spoke to a group of fifty students who were removed from their high school for mostly drug-related offenses. I shared Hayden's troubling story and explained to these kids that Hayden did not have a plan, and neither did we. Not only did I share details about his drug use, but I developed a process for them, and I call it IMAP, which stands for I Make A Plan, and encouraged them to see their life as a journey and to make a map for a safe trip. I reminded them how the dark, rough road they are on now could lead them to a "dead end" like Hayden or to jail. We discussed the bad situations they might find themselves in and how to easily get out of them or how to avoid bad situations completely. Just getting our kids to think and have a plan before they go into the world will help increase their chance for success. Many students do not have family support to help them understand serious issues, such as drugs and legal issues, therefore school is the next best place for young kids to begin their drug-awareness education. Addiction has to be recognized as a disease and better understood by society.

Today our family is healthy and emotionally strong. Our kids are sharing Hayden's story and getting involved in drug-awareness causes. We all have those moments when our emotions stir up tears and we miss him, which I see as emotional scars, or we see pictures of him, which surface our mental scars. Even though we suffered such a tragic loss, I am so glad and feel blessed for the wonderful years we were able to spend with Hayden. I cling to the amazing memories of seeing him for the first time in my arms and the many things I taught him to do while he was growing up. I will cherish all the hugs and kisses he gave me and the laughter we shared. Praying for faith has given me the strength I need to live each day to its fullest. Making choices for the ones we love is much more difficult when we do not understand their condition. We all had to let go of the guilt and shame of our choices to be able to move on with our lives and find peace. Our other kids learned life lessons that will always have an impact on them and will possibly use their knowledge and understanding about addiction to help someone else.

—15—

What We Learned through the Phases of Hayden's Drug Use

We cannot change our past, but I believe by sharing our story, I can help prepare others to have a better understanding and be more informed, in the hope of making the most of their present and better memories of the past.

I discuss the items that I found during the first few years of Hayden's decline with hopes that others can have a better understanding of substance abuse and its progression into addiction. I will also list some issues for thought that could help your family or others around you slow or eliminate drug abuse. The more society understands the disease of addiction, the more lives can be saved. Hayden used marijuana for several years before moving into harder substances such as cocaine and heroin; therefore, I have great concern over states legalizing marijuana, which alters brain function, maturity, motivation, and good judgment. The argument that marijuana should be legal because alcohol is makes no sense. People should be concerned with the number of deaths from drunk driving and alcoholism and not want to legalize another substance that is mind-altering and robs people's motivation. Every rehab meeting we attended to hear drug addicts talk of their past, always began with their first drug—marijuana. They would often describe how after becoming bored with marijuana, they would easily try other drugs for a new feeling. Cough syrups are usually abused with other substances, such as prescription drugs or synthetics. As mentioned earlier, synthetic drugs are legal and sold at smoke shops, also called "head shops," in small, square, decorated packages and usually have some type of cartoon character on them and are named humorously to disguise the drug-like substance that's been packaged. These substances are not monitored or screened by anyone before being sold in these shops, therefore they are very dangerous, and many times, these drugs are laced with other toxins. Synthetics can also lead users into other illegal drugs, so I encourage doing your own research to learn and understand what could be introduced to someone you love.

Heroin use is now an epidemic, and the percentage of people dying from overdose is growing rapidly because it is cheap and easy to buy. I must say I use the word "easy," but some places Hayden went to were dangerous and usually nasty. I still think about the desperation he must have felt to allow himself to be in very rough parts of town. He had a gun put to his head on one occasion as he entered the door and said he felt lucky to have made it out alive. An addict not following a plan to stay clean and using mentor support can quickly decline and not think twice about situations they put themselves in for a fix.

I do believe Hayden may have had a better chance to recover if we allowed him to stay in a long-term recovery facility or even a boarding school when he was young and a few years into his troubles. Leaving him in Montana at a structured boarding school that specialized in teens and drug abuse while getting an education could have changed his life and removed the impact from the rest of the family. We will never know if this could have been a better situation, but I want to encourage others not to feel guilty if you realize your loved one is in need of much more support than you can give, and take into consideration who else is living in your home. We cannot go back in time, so it is important for me to pass this on to any family that could be struggling with an addicted loved one. Many cities are now establishing addiction hotlines to call for help, and counties are establishing drug programs to help citizens in need. Churches around the nation offer NA meetings and AA meetings, which can be found online. There are also non-profit organizations that can help qualifying families cover expenses. Court systems are establishing drug courts for offenders and their families as well.

As for alcohol, when Hayden was clean and we talked, he shared with me how easy alcohol and drugs were to access. Many homes have some type of wet bar in them, usually on display and very easy to access because parents are not monitoring them. I began to think how the drinking age is twenty-one and minors are not allowed to sit at or go into a bar out in public, but yet it is legal to have open bar in our homes. Hayden shared with me that he went into his friends' homes and was able to drink whatever alcohol he wanted because the bottles were lined up on the counter holding hard liquor, wine, and beer. We did not have any type of open bar in our home at the time because the house we lived in did not have an area for that, but as I mentioned in the story, we realized we could not even display wine bottles in our new home. I am just bringing awareness with the hope that if enough people work together, even on small issues, young lives can be changed for the better.

Another huge issue is the abuse of prescription medication such as Xanax, Adderall, OxyContin, and opioids, which are all very addictive. Many times, these medications are prescribed for anxiety, pain, or attention disorders. Hayden was able to use or buy these drugs more than once because of their availability in friends' homes and because they were never locked up or thrown away safely. These medications are only prescribed to adults, and we must be responsible with them. These drugs are most commonly chewed or crushed and snorted through the nose, which is very damaging to the brain. Kids will take and sell these prescription medications at school or on the streets as well, so I am encouraging everyone to keep medications in a safe, secure place and be able to recognize if pills are missing. Below, I discuss the substances I wrote about earlier and the phases to help explain what we noticed about Hayden's progression into drug use.

Phase One began after he desired a quicker high and did not like having to drink a lot of alcohol. In ninth grade, Hayden began drinking because of easy accessibility but did not find drinking in large quantities appealing, therefore after trying marijuana and triggering an enjoyable feeling, he became consumed with that quick high. After about a year, he was introduced to addictive prescription drugs, which I mentioned earlier, for a different type of high and began snorting or chewing crushed pills in addition to smoking. He did feel desperate enough at one time to ingest a bottle of pet anxiety medication, which we had for our dog as needed for her issues, that had a sedative base. Hayden used synthetic drugs such as K2 and ecstasy as well as the deadly bath salts. He eventually experimented with cocaine, but his brain preferred the effects of heroin, which he began shooting up through needles. Heroin is an opioid and therefore increases a release of dopamine in the brain and is one of the hardest drugs to stay clean from. The impact on the brain is very strong, acting as a pain reliever and increasing a feeling of pleasure. Because of its dramatic impact upon first use, many will be drawn back to the damaging substance, and it changes everyone who uses it.

A quick summary of the three phases:

Phase One: lighters, eye drops, white paper squares, clear plastic bags for marijuana purchases

Phase Two: (in addition to Phase One) small glass or metal bong to smoke from, foil for burning and smoking, hollow pens for snorting, others' prescription medication, spoons to heat and melt substances, synthetic drugs sold at smoke shops, also called "head shops" (such as synthetic marijuana called K2), pet anxiety medications

Phase Three: (in addition to Phase Two) cough syrups, bath salts, heroin use and needles

What Does One Do?

SHEA BARAKATT LMSW, LCDC

CLINICAL DIRECTOR—BURNING TREE RANCH

The first answer to the question, "What does one do when they see signs of substance use disorder?" is: Don't ignore it! Don't think that this will go away or that it is just a phase. As a mother of a sixteen-year-old, a recovering alcoholic myself, and a clinical director, these are statements I hear consistently from family members who are seeking solutions for the third, fifth, or fifteenth time to help a loved one who simply will not remain substance free and in recovery (there is a difference).

Having worked with hundreds of clients and families during my career as a therapist, what I can say is this disease is very cunning, baffling, and quite frankly, hard for people to comprehend. I have listened to parents beg, plead, and try to negotiate with loved ones who are actually "insane." The word *insanity* is used because it is termed in the twelve steps of Alcoholics Anonymous. Also, dealing with an individual who is addicted to a substance clearly is not able to function in a sane manner. This is a disease of the mind, body, and spirit, and there should be no negotiating. The addicted individual is so delusional about how they are functioning and truly believe it on some level, as their world is crumbling down around them. Why would we let a delusional individual make decisions for them self when their decisions have ended them up in jails, institutions, or slowly killing themselves by using substances that are destroying them? I see this over and over knowing that the disease is not only consuming the individual but also the family. This is a family disease; everyone plays a part in enabling the disease to be active. The addicted individual ultimately needs the willingness and action to do something different; but the surrounding individuals also need to stop protecting individuals from consequences, feelings; and all the factors that can help propel the desire for change.

Change is never comfortable, so the addicted individual will most always resist change. Working with alcoholics and addicts is very complex; it is not just one influential factor, it is multiple factors all active at one time. We must teach individuals and the family as to "why" the individual uses substances and "why" the family does what they do, such as enabling. We must educate about co-occurring disorders, behaviors, discipline, and mal-adaptive patterns of dealing with life on life terms; along with teaching emotional literacy this can provide the solutions that we know can work. Once the tools are given, it is up to the individual and family to follow through with all the tools, not just using the ones that they want to use. It is very necessary to understand that help and treatment will require time for the addict and the family to heal. When looking for treatment, time is one of the most important factors, and yet families resist placing their loved one in long-term treatment. The National Institute on Drug Abuse defines long-term treatment as six or more months of residential care. Residential care is where long-term care is given in a setting where the individual is living at the facility, receiving clinical services, and supervised by staff twenty-four hours a day. The delusion is that the individual has other things that they need to do or places to go such as school or work. I promise you, anything they place in front of their recovery, they will not be able to successfully accomplish. This is why an addicted loved one should not try recovery in only thirty, sixty, or ninety days. The brain cannot heal, behaviors cannot change, and sobriety tools cannot be learned when a rehab stay is short term. The addicted individual requires much time to not only reinforce tools that can be repeated over and over to become the norm but also for the brain to recover. Behaviors do not change in thirty days of treatment, and the brain does not return to a baseline in thirty days. Depending on the individual's age, substances used, amount used, and duration, it can take up to a full nine months to one year for an individual to be at homeostasis. Also it is vital to have time to deal with trauma, correct medication management for any co-occurring disorders, and to peel away at the layers that have kept the individual and the family sick for so long. The insight and tools one has at two months is significantly lower than at month nine. Success rates increase significantly the longer an individual is in long-term treatment along with completing the program. I will say family sabotage is one of the main reasons for client's leaving long term treatment early. Family members will actually start noticing that the addicted individual sounds and looks better. The addicted individual may start manipulating and saying all the right things, so the family pulls the individual out of treatment believing what they are being told and trusting their enabling minds.

When should families consider long-term treatment? There are good short-term treatment centers; they just do not work for the chronic relapsing client. Some individuals obtain the tools necessary and become responsible, self-supporting, sober individuals after short-term treatment and stay in recovery to live healthy, long lives. If a short-term treatment does not work then why spend the money and try it again? This is what we call "insanity," doing the same thing over and over expecting different results. The answer is, do not keep doing the same thing and expect a different outcome, go to long-term treatment. With substance use disorders, nothing is a perfect answer or a perfect place. There are those clients who do not make it despite every effort from the family and professionals. The client has to be willing and surrendered to the process at some point. This is why we not only encourage but demand for the family to go to Al-Anon, work the steps, and get a sponsor from the very beginning when seeking help. This will not only increase the chances for the addicted individual, but what if the loved one does not recover? Co-dependency can kill the loved ones just like the substances kill the individual using them, only slower. Al-Anon is a program to help individuals dealing with an addicted individual recover them self regardless of what the addicted individual does with their life.

Knowing the family of the author of this book, I was asked to share my experience on what to look for when substances might be suspected (alcohol and drugs are all in the same and work on the same reward centers in the brain). Having a teenager myself, the first thing I have done since my son was old enough to understand is education, education, education! Every time I hear of an overdose or death from alcohol poisoning, I tell him. I allow and encourage random drug testing (he is an athlete, and I love when they get tested). When teenagers return home at night, always have a conversation with them to check appearance and breath, and look for dilated pupils. I share with him his biology and his probability of being addicted to a substance, food, sex, or anything. I tell people to always lock up alcohol and addictive medications if in the home. Most teenagers get pills and alcohol from the home they live in or their friends' homes. Doctors that we trust prescribe addictive medications at an alarming rate. Doctors should be individuals we trust, but we must do our homework. Parents need to educate themselves on what medications are addictive or have what we call as "street value." Antibiotics do not have any "street value" because they do not change one's mood, for example. Most people today ignore the warning signs. There are telling signs of what I call the "isms," being irritable, restless, and discontent. There are behaviors that go along with alcoholism and addiction even if the individual is not putting substances in their body. The real unmanageability is the "ism" Some things to look for:

1. Lying
2. Hoarding or problems with money
3. Extreme change in mood
4. Change in social activities
5. Change in friends
6. Breaking the law
7. Sleeping too much or too little
8. Being sick a lot
9. Dilated pupils
10. Erratic, impulsive behavior
11. Staying away from home a lot
12. Problems with education or work
13. Auto accidents
14. Blaming others for all their problems
15. Getting into fights
16. Change in diet, eating a lot or very little

These are a few of the things that are important to notice in an individual. Teenagers can be tough sometimes because there are some of these things that are normal aspects of growing up. People do go through tough times with school and work and blame others for their problems. Does this mean they are using substances? Not always, but it is a good idea to get to the root of the problem and seek help. My son is very moody and independent, and he likes to call the shots, but this is where I get to check out any suspicions. I am his parent, not his friend. He can be mad at me all he wants! Some people are afraid to rock the boat with their loved ones. This does more harm than good and is a selfish act by not wanting to deal with a problem. I do not claim to be the know-it-all therapist or mother, and there are days I truly believe some decisions I made were not the best for my son. At the end of the day this is where Al-Anon and working the twelve steps with sponsors (yes I have two: Al-Anon and Alcoholics Anonymous) can save my sanity and sobriety. It is hard not to enable our children or loved ones, but we must ask ourselves "what is going on with me that I feel so out of control right now and I feel awful?" Are you doing something for someone who is perfectly capable of doing it themselves? Are you afraid that you might make someone upset? Well, the good news is that every individual is responsible for their own feelings and behaviors, including yourself. We cannot make someone feel anything and vice versa. I always say "no" is a complete sentence, and I stick to this. Saying no is hard for some individuals to do, along with not carrying the guilt.

In America today, we have a real epidemic going on that is killing our loved ones at an unbelievable rate. In the many years I have been counseling addicts and their families, the problem is not only getting worse, but the substances keep changing. It is vital to know what we are dealing with, to help educate, and to do what we can, not only for the individuals we love, but for ourselves as well. Families these days have so much more to compete with, such as the internet, social media, video games, smartphones, and all other technology that most of us never had as teenagers or young adults. Because mental health is changing, know what you are dealing with, even if you do not have a loved one dealing with substance abuse disorders. Someone close to you could be struggling, and the better educated we all are, the better chance society has to decrease the number of addicts.

Burning Tree Admissions

866-287-2877

P.O. Box 757

Kaufman, Texas 75142

www.BurningTree.com

WebIntake@BurningTree.com

Shea Barakatt LMSW, LCDC

972-962-7374

SNBarakatt@BurningTree.com

About the Author

Susán Hoemke knows firsthand what it's like to have a loved one who is struggling with addiction. A wife and mother of four, her life took an unexpected turn in the form of her son Hayden's addiction and other subsequent family tragedies that taught her—the hard way—the challenges of living with this disease. Now she hopes not only to bring awareness and understanding to drug addiction but also to offer hope and healing after loss. Her research, experience attending rehab meetings, and time spent living with an addicted love one enable her to speak on this subject from a deeply personal perspective. Today, Hoemke is a public speaker and the owner of a product development company. She lives in Dallas, Texas, with her husband, Carl, and youngest daughter, Olivia, while her other two adult children, Landon and Miranda, live in Austin.

As a boy, Hayden enjoyed family, friends, and meeting new people. He was full of humor and wit and therefore had a great ability to bring laughter to an entire room. An A student through eighth grade, Hayden's creativity always made his work unique and interesting when he was assigned a project. He also had a special passion for music and a gift for lyricism. Before his death, he attended the Art Institute of Dallas in the hope of earning his degree in audio engineering. Hayden is missed by the many people who love him. The knowledge that Hayden is resting peacefully now in God's care brings comfort to his family and friends, who all look forward to seeing him again someday. He is gone but never forgotten.